# MINDSTORMS

## 25 EXERCISES TO
## DISCOVER YOUR INNER
## ENTREPRENEUR

# KATHLEEN CELMINS

*Mindstorms: 25 Exercises to Discover Your Inner Entrepreneur*
Copyright ©2021 by Kathleen Celmins

Paperback: ISBN: 978-1-7379186-0-8
eBook: ISBN: 978-1-7379186-1-5
Library of Congress Control Number: 2021918805

Editors: D. Olson Pook and Emma Bates
Cover & Interior Design: Fusion Creative Works, fusioncw.com

Printed in the United States of America
First Edition

*For Brent, who made time for this book
to be written. Who was the first set of eyes
other than my own to see this in its raw form and
helped make it better. Who is the best person to wake
up to every morning, and not just because
he makes the coffee.*

# CONTENTS

## PART 4: BUILDING YOUR MARKETING ENGINE

## PART 5: FUELING YOUR MARKETING ENGINE

# INTRODUCTION

One Friday morning three years ago, I found myself in a house in Paradise Valley, a ritzy suburb of Phoenix. It really did feel like paradise, too. The house I'd rented was nestled on what had to be an acre of land. There was a pool outside, an outdoor fireplace, and a hot tub. Add the spacious bedrooms and gourmet kitchen and we were staying inside the kind of dream home you find in travel magazines.

I was there hosting a three-day "Mindshop" to help three people tap into their inner entrepreneur. As part of my business at amplifiedNOW, I regularly led these Mindshops, sharing the ins and outs of leveraging the internet to build a marketing engine to drive businesses built around great ideas.

Earlier, we shared a small breakfast in the kitchen and now people were chatting. It was time to get started. I rinsed dishes, put them in the dishwasher, and set the coffee to brew one more time. I looked up at f the women who had gathered.

The looks on their faces made it clear just how much it took each of them to show up today.

They were nervous and excited. Four strangers, all in on this retreat, but none of them were sure what, exactly, they could expect from the weekend. The looks on their faces and the fact that conversation didn't come easily made me realize one thing.

It was time.

"Good morning, everyone!" I said. "Let's move into the living room area. I think there's plenty of space for everyone to sit. Help yourself to coffee and water and make yourselves comfortable. We'll have plenty of breaks throughout the day." Everyone went into the living room and made themselves comfortable. I started my speech.

"I have a feeling I know why you showed up this weekend. You've seen the success stories. Your best friend's sister's cousin launched a course and made six figures in a week. Someone else you sort-of know had virtually no presence online one day and is now pulling in more money than they could ever spend."

They looked at each other. Did one of the women raise her eyebrows? We were off to a good start.

"There are so many examples of turning the internet into an ATM with unlimited withdrawal opportunities, so it might seem like there's no room for your idea. That maybe all the money-making ideas have already been taken. That there's no room for you. That it's too little, too late. That if only you'd started some time ago, you could be successful. But not now." I looked up. "Has anyone here thought those thoughts?"

They nodded. "Good. Because the first thing I get to tell you is that you're wrong. Sure, you can't do what was done two, five, ten years ago, but that doesn't mean all the money in the world has been spent. In fact, think of the people you've heard about as the trailblazers. Because they paved the way for people like you," I said, pointing at the woman to my left, "and you, and you — to turn what you know into a business. Trust me when I say, we are at the **very beginning** of making money on the internet. We are standing in shade because those who came before us planted a tree."

## A CRYSTAL BALL

Let me step out of the Mindshop for a moment to repeat that thought.

We are at *the very beginning* of making money on the internet.

What do I mean?

Allow me to dust off my crystal ball and predict the future. Let me briefly paint a scene.

It's the future and the kids of today are adults. Some of them are old enough to have kids of their own. A few of them are sitting around a kitchen table reminiscing about the good old days.

"Remember when shipping took more than one day? When things arrived in boxes versus being printed at home?"

"Remember when all the TV shows were on different streaming platforms?"

"Remember learning to drive? Or actually driving ourselves places?"

"When people... typed?"

"We really thought we were living in the future then, but we didn't have a clue."

They chuckle, chew on their alkalized water, then dial-up their personalized holoview — what their parents' generation quaintly referred to as "workstations."

That's enough of my crystal ball for now. Because it turns out that those who can think have a crystal ball of their own. It's called their mind.

Anyone with a mind can predict this with certainty: The world will look vastly different in just one generation than it does today.

Commuting will be something we do to meet in person — not something we do to get to work.

We'll exercise differently, live where it makes the most sense without any regard to where "the office" is, and have friends all over the world.

And more and more activities that would have required going places will take place online. We'll be doing so much more online, both for work and for pleasure. What started as a necessary way to stay safe during a global pandemic will have far-reaching consequences.

Moving activities online will free up time we would have wasted, but so will advances in automation. Robots already clean our floors, but they'll get better at it, and we'll see many of our routine tasks outsourced to robots and other AI.

Pretty much everything we know will change — except one thing.

The one thing that still resists the onslaught of change is the same thing that makes it all possible.

The human mind.

Because while we can shift activities online and automate strength, we can't do either to knowledge, insight, or inspiration.

This book isn't about whether the rise of the robot is a good thing or a bad thing or whether the shift to an online economy is better or worse than the good old days. After all, any change is going to involve both the good and the bad.

What this book is about is showing you that the future belongs to those of us who can think.

Let's rejoin the story for a bit.

## A SIMPLE IMAGE

"We're going to cover a lot this weekend, and this image will help."

I passed out a diagram of a three-legged stool. On each leg there were words. The first was *expertise*. The second was *positioning*. And on the third was *marketing engine*.

"See how it's a three-legged stool? If one leg of a stool is longer or shorter than the others, it doesn't work. And if one is missing, then everything falls apart. That's exactly what it's like to turn your ideas into a business."

"Over the next three days we're going to do some exercises to help you figure out:

- Your areas of expertise
- How to position your expertise into things that will make you the most money; and
- How to create the marketing engine you need to build to make it all happen.

"We'll get to all of these throughout the rest of the weekend but let me give you a little preview."

"First, your areas of expertise. We'll do a series of exercises — what I call *Mindstorms* — where we'll figure out what we know."

"Then, we'll talk about the best ways to position yourself, and your expertise, to help the most people, and make the biggest impact."

"Finally, we'll talk about how to put it all together in the simplest way possible, so we don't end up doing work that feels like work but doesn't actually move the needle."

"Each of these legs is equally important, hence the stool. You need to have solid expertise, great positioning, and a clear way to bring more money to make this work, and we'll spend time over this Mindshop getting clear on all three legs."

"Unless there are any questions, let's get to introductions. Why don't you tell us your name and a description of what you think your area of expertise is."

"I'll start," I said. "My name is Kathleen Celmins and I'm a marketing strategist for digital entrepreneurs. My expertise is in marketing and creating systems for busy entrepreneurs and small businesses so that they can make more money from the internet. I help people just like you figure out how."

## FROM THERE TO HERE

Let me jump in here again. Maybe you've heard there's money to be made on the internet. Maybe you're even interested in claiming your slice of it?

To that I say, heck freaking yes. There *is* money to be made on the internet and you can have your piece of it. Pinky swear.

How do I know? Perhaps it's time for a slightly longer introduction.

I've been working online in some capacity since 2011, which in internet years is a Very Long Time Indeed. I jumped into the wild world of online business through personal finance. I wrote about my journey into and out of a mountain of consumer debt. The writing was that of an amateur, the structure was nonexistent, but the heart was there. Some posts were so vulnerable it was as if I'd cut open a vein and bleed on the page (or screen as it were). Some were terrible. Many were both.

I found my voice and my community in the online personal finance world, building my blog up to a point where I thought I would really capture some of the *vast amounts of money flowing* around online. Back then, you got more attention from Google by constantly publishing fresh material. So, I published five, six, sometimes seven articles a week (oh, let's not call them articles!).

And I did gain attention. My page views were climbing. I was becoming known. My stuff was starting to show up on the first page of search results. And my peers, who'd started their blogs just six months before me, were making upwards of $50,000 *per month* on private ads.

At the time there was a loophole in the Google search algorithm. All a person had to do to get on the first page of search results was to get a bunch of sites linking to their site no matter the quality or relevance of the link. It was quite a loophole.

Getting on the first page of Google results was as lucrative then as it is today. Of course, there's little reason why a personal finance blog would link to an online casino, so sketchy companies paid thousands of dollars — sometimes tens of thousands of dollars — for people to write about nothing even remotely related to their site and link to it. The strategy worked well.

Thankfully for all of us who search the internet multiple times a day, Google closed the loophole sometime in the middle of 2012. The first page of search results now contains links that are all *highly relevant* to whatever it is you want to find online.

But the algorithm update also changed the way business was run online. Instead of making money hand over fist, sites with those sketchy links were demoted. Page one? Forget it. They didn't even make it to page 20 of search results.

So, before I even had to consider if I was the kind of person who would accept $10,000 for a link from an online casino or a payday loan company, the "sketchy link buying" business model imploded and that line of income dried up for me and everyone else in my corner of the internet.

Once the dust settled, everyone had to figure out what to do next. Some people left. Some stayed around. But no one made money from paid link placements from online casinos anymore.

As for me, I was hooked, and I was starting to develop my expertise. I started developing my writing muscle, and I got really interested in the idea of making money online. I wanted a practical, strategic approach to making money, and I found it through marketing.

My last corporate job was a work-from-home marketing position, which helped solidify the idea that there was money to be made online, it was just a matter of fine-tuning my expertise and using positioning to gain authority.

I partnered with a popular personal finance podcast and made them profitable. Once I realized my calling was marketing, not personal finance, I knew it was time for me to pivot.

I wanted to make more brands profitable, and marketing was the way. So I sold back my shares of the business to my partners and wished them good things. In the spring of 2018, I decided to go all-in and become a marketing strategist.

What's a marketing strategist, you ask? The best way to explain is to show you. Read on and find out!

## MEET THE MINDSTORMERS

"Who would like to go next?"

All three pairs of eyes were on me. I thought that was a good sign. Over my last retreat, when I asked people to introduce themselves, everyone in the room was looking at the floor. Not this group.

I looked at the woman sitting cross-legged in the chair to my left. "Why don't you start us off?"

"Okay," she nodded. "My name is Yosi, and I'm a Human Resources assistant. I don't know what my expertise is, but it's not in HR, I know that." She looked at the woman to her left, but I wasn't going to let her off the hook so quickly.

"Later we will do Mindstorming exercises so you can hone in on your core areas of expertise, but let me ask you Yosi, when you say 'definitely not' HR, what do you mean by that?"

"Well," she said, then paused. "It's just that... actually, I don't dislike the work itself — I do find some satisfaction in getting all the paperwork together and putting a bow on it, so to speak. I just hate the environment at my office, and I feel like I'm counting the hours until 5:30, then counting the days until Friday, and I'm not even 30 yet and I know there has to be more to life than this."

I nodded. "Thanks for opening up and clarifying. We'll keep those desires in mind this weekend as we explore your expertise."

I turned to the woman directly to Yosi's left.

"Hi, I'm Michelle. I am a stay-at-home mom, but my youngest is starting kindergarten in the fall, and I want to get back to making money. The thing is, I'm not interested in going to work on someone else's terms. I have a background in corporate communications, but I'm not sure how that translates into anything we're discussing here."

I smiled. "I hear you — and I'm glad you're here, Michelle."

Then I turned to the third woman and nodded. She said, "I'm so glad to be here. My name is Jackie, and I teach yoga. My expertise is in yoga. I have over 800 hours of teacher training, but, like Michelle, I don't know how that expertise translates online. Who cares how flexible I am in cyberspace?"

Everyone laughed.

"Funny that you say that," I said. "The truth is, everyone has that same thought about their own expertise. The things that come naturally to us don't feel like they have much value because even though we might have worked on them for hundreds of hours, the fact that they come naturally to us now, they're not seen as very special. But the opposite is true, and that's what we'll spend the rest of today working on. But I'm getting ahead of myself."

## THE LIFE OF A MARKETING STRATEGIST

Before I do get too far ahead, let me tell you what it's like *being* a marketing strategist. I help companies craft their digital marketing strategies. We come up with ideas for their next campaign, brainstorm marketing ideas, and help amplify their expertise without them having to spend too much time in the marketing trenches. Amplifying a brand's expertise helps solidify the first leg on the stool. In fact, a solid marketing strategy is the stool itself: expertise, positioning, and a marketing engine that helps create the cycle of profitability for the long term.

One of my superpowers is looking at someone's business and finding three to five easy opportunities for increasing their subscriber count and, more importantly, their revenue.

Now, a bit about the format of this book. We're going to follow the three women you just met through a three-day workshop (from now on, we'll use my term 'Mindshop') divided into five parts where they'll navigate their way through a Mindshop weekend and create the foundation for their knowledge-based business. There are exercises, Mindstorming sessions, and various other tools that we use throughout the workshop, and you're invited to follow along.

This is a fictional example of a real-life weekend Mindshop I run several times a year. You're welcome to join one of our live events — there's really nothing like the power of an in-person retreat. But that's not feasible for everyone, so if you're the type of person who's in a similar place as the people you just read about, go through the exercises on your own time.

If you're anything like my business partner, Emma Bates, COO of amplifiedNOW, you're going to get stuck on how to implement each mindstorm. As I tell her in every mindstorm we run together, put aside the mechanics of how you'll get something off the ground. Allow your future self (or your future Emma) to handle the how. Over the course of this book, focus on what you're doing, and why.

The best way to treat this book is to read the examples, then set aside time to go through the exercises on your own. The exercises included are often simple Mindstorming tools. But don't be fooled by their simplicity. The most simple tools are often the most powerful. You can follow the narrative, but more than that, you can experience the narrative — you'll be prompted to write for 15 minutes just like when the characters write for 15 minutes, taking notes in your own notebook (or you can download an accompanying workbook from MINDSTORMSbook.com and use its pre-formatted pages to guide you as you read).

Because this follows a narrative, it's set to finish in three days. But it's a lot to cover in three days, and even when we run these workshops in person, attendees are often exhausted by the end. Don't feel like you must finish the book in three days — you can set your own pace. It's why it's been divided into five parts for you.

As you'll also see as you read on, all the tools and exercises are intended to be jumping-off points. You need to spend more than three days building a business around the ideas, thoughts, and knowledge you possess, of course. Each part needs more time and attention from you to bring your ideas to fruition. But it's a good start.

So, if you want to download ideas from your brain, think about income differently, and build a marketing engine for your new business, grab the workbook at MINDSTORMSbook.com and follow along. If you simply want to read a story about people going through a workshop, that's fine too.

The point is to get you thinking about the possibilities that exist. The value is absorbing, then doing the same exercises the characters do, *as they're going through it.*

This book is intended to help you figure out what you know, what makes you stand out, and what you can build. You don't need a 1000-page journey. You need just enough to show your ideas (however they seem to you) are enough to make money online.

If you're not convinced yet, let me share just the last little bit of that first hour of the Mindshop from three years ago.

## FIRST HOUR: GROUND RULES

It was time to spell out the ground rules for the weekend.

I hung a poster on that wall that read, "Love what you do, and you'll never work a day in your life" in a nice script font.

I stood next to it and waited a beat longer than was comfortable. All eyes were on me.

Pointing to the poster, I said, "This quote is one of *the most damaging* quotes I've ever run across. It implies that if you search long enough and hard enough you will find a career and a life that somehow doesn't feel like work. If I had a physical soapbox, I would be standing on it right now because this simply couldn't be further from the truth. Expecting work to feel like play means you are going to be the cat chasing a laser pointer. The chase is fun, but even when you catch it, you're not going to catch it. So, for our purposes here, let's turn this poster around."

I turned it so the text faced the wall and continued.

"The truth is, you have to *love* the work when you're building a business around your knowledge. Instead of chasing the laser pointer, you start with your foundation and work harder than you've worked in your life. But that's not as fun as a poster. So, I'll leave it blank. Because what we're doing is *so much bigger* than what would fit on a poster."

# THE 5 MINDSHOP AGREEMENTS

I handed out a sheet of paper titled *The 5 Mindshop Agreements*.

"Instead, I'd like for you to agree with me on the following statements."

**"One: It's okay not to know my five-year plan.** In fact, it's better not to have one, or at least not have one that is set in stone because in many ways we don't know much about what will happen five years from now, except that we'll be five years older."

**"Two: I have all the knowledge and expertise I need right inside me.** There's a temptation to learn more, go back to school, get some credentials, some external validation that you can position yourself as an expert. But you don't need it. You have everything you need to be successful right inside you. The rest of these mindstorms will show you this."

**"Three: Becoming an expert is a matter of positioning.** Since you have all the knowledge and expertise inside you, the missing piece is how to position yourself so you're trading your time for more money. You could make about ten times more money hosting a half-day workshop than you could make writing a well-researched blog post."

**"Four: Commercial success is *not* passive.** There's no magic combination of expertise and positioning that will make the money come without marketing. You have to be aggressive to achieve success."

**"Five: Success isn't just for other people, it's for me too.** To be successful, you must believe (and not just believe, work toward!) that success is possible for you. Some people are making money using the same knowledge that you have. None of them are somehow more special than you are. Nothing good comes from falling into the comparison trap. The only difference between you and your visions of success is some combination of positioning and marketing."

"This is a personal contract. If everyone agrees, please sign and date this document. This is going to be amazing, and by signing your names, you're agreeing to let this weekend open your mind."

They all signed their papers and returned them to me.

Dear reader, I'm going to act like you've signed that piece of paper, too.

Typically, when you sign something you get something in return. You're promising me that you'll keep an open mind over the next 200 or so pages.

What do you get in return?

You get an iron-clad guarantee from me.

What is it?

Your success is **inevitable**.

Before you roll your eyes, let me explain. I'm going to show you what's possible.

Write this down on a piece of paper and put it somewhere you can see it: **My success is inevitable.**

Because your success *is* inevitable. Decide what you're going to work toward. Your work ethic, your intelligence, your strength of mind, your stick-to-it-iveness, your willingness to keep trying new things when one doesn't pan out — those are all traits of highly successful people, both offline and on.

Success is not inevitable for everyone. But it is for you.

Throughout the rest of this book, I'll show you how. Let's start by really understanding what it is you know.

# PART 1:

# DOWNLOAD YOUR MIND

# DISCOVERING YOUR EXPERTISE

It's time for the first Mindstorm exercise, both for you, dear reader, and the attendees of the Mindshop. It's a long one, so get yourself in a comfortable spot, grab a cup of coffee or tea and open your notebook. You might even want to have some different colored pens for organizing your thoughts.

Are you ready? Can you set aside the next 30 minutes? I think it's important to finish this once you get started, and it's going to take around half an hour, so don't start till you can lock in and focus.

Ok then — here we go! Turn to page one of the Mindstorms Exercise book, found at MINDSTORMSbook.com.

The point of this first exercise is to figure out exactly *what you know*. I am going to start by giving you prompts and asking you to write down the first few things that pop into your head. This is just for you, so don't worry about impress-

29

ing someone or making yourself look good — it's better if you just answer as honestly and frankly as you can. Give yourself the space to write freely. I find that a Mindstorm like this is best done when I'm sleepy — either first thing in the morning or after a long day — that way, my inner critic is tired, too.

Once you finish writing I'll show you what the other three people wrote down so you can get a sense of how different people's answers can be. If you're ever stuck or needing inspiration when doing a Mindstorm on your own, you're always welcome to read ahead. Be true to yourself in your answers — it's your thoughts you're after, not someone else's.

At the top of your piece of paper, write the word **FIELDS**. (If you've downloaded the workbook, you have these sheets preformatted for you). Now write down the subjects you studied in school. Majors, minors, classes you took that you liked, things you concentrated on in high school even — the stuff that's still in your head. Be thorough, but don't kick yourself if you can't recall every single detail. Spend about five minutes on this.

Write a second big heading: **PROFICIENCIES**. This time jot down the things you're proficient in. We're ultimately after your expertise, but we're not there yet. All I'm asking for here are the things that you didn't study in school but dig into simply for the joy of learning. Think of the topics that fascinate you. They can be anything:

- Dating

- Marriage

- Parenting

- Any of your hobbies
- Any of your chores
- Any topic you originally *had* to learn about for yourself or someone you love, like navigating healthcare for seniors or Social Security
- The section at the bookstore or library where you're always drawn to or have read the most from

Think of the things that you could teach someone who doesn't know ANYTHING about that topic. What are the topics you could teach — to children, to beginners, to intermediate-level learners?

Give yourself five minutes and write them all down — and remember, there are no bad answers in Mindstorming.

The next heading I want you to write is **ADVISOR.** This time I want you to think about what you're good at from the lens of what other people think.

What are the things people in your life come to you to get help with? Think about your coworkers and colleagues, but also your friends and neighbors. What things do you know better than your peers? Let me help jog your memory:

- Are you the Excel expert in your department?
- The organizational master of your friend group?
- Maybe the photographer of your family?
- Are you asked to sing at weddings?

31

- Are you the person who gets tasked with writing eulogies?

- Would everyone be upset if you didn't make your special homemade caramels every Christmas? (That one might be just me).

Think hard now: what seemingly mundane things can you do that you think are so ordinary that when you see someone else struggling, you have a hard time understanding why they struggle? Take a little longer this time to list them all — somewhere between 5 and 10 minutes.

But use that time to really think about things. Everyone has a writing face whether it's scrunched up or smiling. And get over yourself if you think that the page needs to be pristine: don't be afraid to write and cross things out, so long as you keep writing!

Treat this as a free writing exercise and don't stop for the entire time. Some of your best stuff — your talents that are so innate you've barely even recognized that they are talents — won't come out until you put this stuff down on the page.

The next list is going to be one that you'll refer to time and time again. The heading for this one is **PERSONALITY DNA**. It'll take a bit more time to complete as well because I want you to go deep into yourself.

What I want you to put down on the page are the things that are unique about you. What are your quirks? What are the "*so you*" things that other people don't get? These are the flavors of your personality. The things which, combined, distinguish you from the Michelles or Yosis or Jackies of the world. Each on its own maybe doesn't feel special, but when taken together makes up the DNA of your distinct personality.

To make this easier — but also to make it more thorough — break this list into several categories:

- Identity
  - Your birth order
  - Where you grew up
  - The number of siblings you have
- Habits
  - How you take your coffee
  - How picky of an eater you are
  - The kinds of exercises you do or do not do
  - Whether you're a morning person or a night owl
- Personality
  - The number of things that make you laugh
  - Your relationship to religion
  - Your pet peeves

Again, we're circling around your expertise but not tackling it head-on.

You literally wouldn't be able to see your expertise if you approached it head-on. This crab-like movement toward the truth is much more likely to produce the outcome we want.

So what am I trying to get you to tell yourself with these categories? I'm trying to get you to explain what you identify with, your habits, and your personality. Doing so will *enhance* the way you approach whatever it is you ultimately land on for your expertise.

Now for the final exercise of the first Mindstorm. Like any good facilitator, I saved the best for last — and it also happens to be my favorite of the bunch.

At the top of the next page write **PASSIONS**. In this section, write about the topics you love — even if they're not the topics you're the MOST proficient in. I'm talking about topics that you could talk about for 30 minutes without coming up for air because you simply love them.

Focus on your passions. Not just what you could teach to others, but the topics you have a soapbox for preaching on. Maybe you love meditation but don't see yourself teaching it — onto the list it goes.

Don't pause to justify your passions — all you need to do is list the ones you have. Why do you have strong opinions about fountain pens and notebook paper? Now's not the time to explain. Now's the time to jot down all the things you could get up and discuss with someone who shares your passion or is interested in learning more — 30 minutes more — about it. Take another five to ten minutes — think hard and list all your passions.

Now comes the fun part. Look at all the things on your lists. Flip back and forth and refamiliarize yourself with what you wrote down earlier compared to what you just spelled out. Now circle the ones that came up on more than one list. Circle the ones that make you smile. Circle the topics that you could see building your name around.

We're starting to narrow down on your area of expertise. Just like everyone who takes one of my Mindshops, you're going to circle or highlight more than one topic. In fact, it's common to have a list of seven or eight topics after this exercise. We're not looking for "the one" here, but we are looking to narrow your list from 39.

Write down all your circled topics on a new sheet of paper. Are there any that go together? Is one a subset of another? It's important to recognize any possible connections, so instead of using your mental 'delete' key and ruling out anything you circled, put it on the new page. Don't be shy — it all matters. Start to rearrange the things that came out of your mind. Create a mind map if yours is the kind of brain that thinks in terms of mind maps. Draw lines connecting topics or start fresh on a new sheet and create new lists. And just because a topic is connected to another doesn't mean it can't connect to a third or fourth.

If you're stuck, an easy way to get started is to just pick one or two topics from each section that resonate with you the most. Then see if the other things you've circled fit with them. Don't be afraid to change your mind mid-way through the process about where the "hot spots" are. Invest the time to imagine connections where none at first glance might appear.

You'll end up with one or two topics in each of these categories:

- Fields

- Proficiencies

- Advisor

- Personality DNA

- Passions

You'll know you're done when you can look at that list and smile at every topic on it. Don't make your list too narrow — you want plenty of options to explore. If you have any questions, read the next section and see what Michelle, Yosi, and Jackie arrived at to see what I'm after for you.

## FIRST MINDSTORM RESULTS

After taking Michelle, Yosi, and Jackie through all the steps of the first Mindstorm, I looked around and asked, "Who wants to share what they've discovered?"

There was a pause. I waited, knowing that if I waited long enough, someone would volunteer their results.

I didn't have to wait long.

Michelle, the stay-at-home mom, said, "I'll go first. This was a helpful exercise for me because it had me asking questions that I haven't asked myself in a long time."

She looked at me. "Should I just talk about each category?"

I nodded. She said, "Okay, here's what I came up with,"

"The FIELDS I find myself drawn to the most are business and communications."

"My PROFICIENCIES are about creating memories with your kids and making healthy dinners that everyone will eat."

"In the ADVISOR list, I came up with quick house cleaning ideas. It seems like everyone is always asking me for ideas about tidying up their house!"

"The more interesting parts of my PERSONALITY DNA are my relationship with my family and the fact that I have an identical twin."

"My PASSIONS are my kids, of course, but also mosaic art. I just love how you can create something wonderful from something broken."

She looked up. "That's it. It doesn't seem like much to me."

I nodded. "It won't. Because what you know rarely seems that impressive from where you're sitting. But I perked up and wanted to know more about how to create memories, how to make healthy dinners, and how you approach life as a twin. I can't speak for everyone else here, but my curiosity is piqued! Thanks for going first."

I turned to Yosi. "Do you want to go next?"

She shook her head. "I don't know. My topics seem so… insignificant."

Let me jump in before continuing to tell you about Yosi's results with an observation about Yosi's remark. I want to pause for a second because there's a little bit of Yosi in all of us.

A comment like hers comes up every time I run one of these workshops. Every time. For whatever reason, several of us have gotten into our heads the idea that taking the time to discuss the significance of our ideas isn't important.

It usually is framed the way Yosi said it — that the ideas aren't that good. But in fact, that's never the problem. It's not that Yosi's (or your) ideas are small because if we're being totally honest here all ideas are small if you think about it. It's that they're our ideas — and our opinion of ourself is actually what's so small.

The problem in other words is the voice in your head telling you that *you're* wrong, *your* ideas won't work, and *you* don't have what it takes. The same ideas in the head of someone else would be fine — it's really you that is the problem.

It reminds me of a cartoon I once saw:

© marketoonist.com

What a lot of people face are deep self-esteem issues. I won't pretend that a Mindshop directed at tapping one's inner entrepreneur can also solve someone's self-esteem issues. But I can promise this: by the end of this book, you won't think so poorly about your ideas — *your* ideas — and hence probably will improve your estimation of yourself as well. This is one of those "you're going to have to trust me moments" — but it's true.

You're going to have to suspend judgment of yourself and therefore your ideas. When you allow your ideas to freely flow out onto the page, you're simply recording your thoughts. There's really no point in judging them (and I certainly haven't asked you to judge them either when I told you to circle them). They're just ideas.

They're not even business ideas (yet). But it's when people start categorizing and evaluating them that they get ahead of themselves. They try to picture turning one of these ideas into a full-fledged business and begin to scoff at the very thought of it (even though the ink isn't even dry on the list yet!).

For every idea that you think is too small, I bet you I can find an example of someone doing something very similar and making a ton of money doing it.

So hold off on making value judgments about our ideas and get back to the task of just cataloging ideas to see if there are any patterns that emerge.

Here's what I told Yosi, framed in terms of the idea of imposter syndrome, which is loosely defined as doubting your abilities and feeling like a fraud:

"It's normal to think your ideas are small, but that's imposter syndrome rearing its ugly head, telling you there's not a place for you at the table. Imposter syndrome tells you that your ideas are not good enough, or worse, that if they are good enough, other people have already executed on them, better than you ever would. Or that your ideas are too big, too small, too vanilla, too out there. Or it's too late."

"Imposter syndrome asks you who the heck do you think you are, trying to do this."

"That voice is wrong."

"But to find that place, you need to stop judging your ideas and just look at them. All we're doing here right now is just sorting through them like they were baseball cards. And you can sort them like baseball cards in a dozen different ways — by team, by position, by batting average, etc. ... we're just taking in all the different patterns that emerge."

"Yosi, does that help?"

She still looked hesitant, but she said, "yes, I think I can share."

"My FIELD was the humanities."

"My PROFICIENCIES are in grammar and spelling — I'm actually a whiz at both."

"As an ADVISOR, what I came up with is how I give these video gifts to my friends and they are always asking for more."

"Some of the more interesting parts of my PERSONALITY DNA include that I like trying new foods and I'm obsessed with my skincare routine."

"And my PASSIONS come through in my ability to talk for half an hour about Instagram filters, PokemonGO, fountain pens, and hand lettering."

"See what I mean about these ideas being small?" Yosi said as she turned to me expectantly.

"I do see where you might think that," I told her. "But I have to tell you that none of those ideas are small. And for me, at least several are quirky and original — fountain pens and hand lettering! And we're still at the very beginning of the weekend. You might be surprised at where your ideas go from here."

"But I do want to acknowledge your worries and not brush them aside. And let me be very clear to all of you. I don't know how Mindstorming ever got the reputation that it's anything close to anyone's idea of fun. I feel like at least once per session I end up writing some version of I DON'T KNOW ANYTHING, I'VE NEVER KNOWN ANYTHING, AND IT'S AMAZING I'VE LIVED SO LONG IN THE WORLD HAVING LEARNED SO LITTLE. And if you're not feeling that way, don't worry — it's early yet!"

She smiled and I smiled.

"But we're not done here — not by a long shot. Now Jackie, are you ready?"

Jackie said, "Thank you for saying what you said, Yosi because I thought I was the only one. I can't tell you how much of a comfort it is to know that I'm not alone in thinking that the Mindstorming session yielded nothing but tumbleweeds."

"Here I go,"

"I double-majored in English and Spanish when I was in college. Like I mentioned before, I'm proficient in yoga and I'm trained in Reiki as well. I also have proficiencies in energy and vibration work, which can be tricky to explain, but it means I can really get a read on someone even if I'm not in the same room as they are. You'd think that people would come to me for advice about their emotional state, and I suppose they do, but more often than not I'm seriously approached by people asking for advice about paint colors for their walls. My personality DNA is vegan, hippie, crunchy, and natural — no surprise there. And I can talk all day long about the impact we have on one another's days. The power of doing something nice, the impact of a kind word or phrase, the science behind cultivating a practice for joy."

"That's what I came up with."

"That's a great list, Jackie. Thank you for sharing."

"Now we're closer to identifying our expertise — or to be more precise, we're closer to narrowing down to the very beginning of our area of expertise. I love what you've shared. Now it's time to start narrowing down our lists. Is everyone ready?"

Everyone nodded.

## CREATING CATEGORIES

Stepping back from the narrative for a second, the next step is to take stock holistically of where you stand. To borrow a photography metaphor, it's time to zoom out to capture the whole picture. This will not be easy because you're just not well-positioned to do this.

Think of it this way: you are like wine inside a bottle. From where you are you can tell me quite a lot about yourself: your color, vintage, acidity, what you pair well with, and not just the varietal of grapes that compose your blend but the exact field each grape came from.

What you can't tell is what your label looks like. And you can't tell whether you are top shelf, bottom shelf, or somewhere in between. You can't tell me if you're at a fancy wine shop or a gas station. All you can do is look at the other wine bottles near you and see what their labels look like.

One thing that might feel reassuring to you is that none of the other bottles can see their own labels either. Their context is the same as yours: partial, at best.

The trick then is to pop your cork, let yourself breathe, and take in your new surroundings. It's easier to do that if you watch someone else "pour a glass" if you will, so let's rejoin our story and watch how Yosi discovers her label.

"To begin, we're going to find an overarching category for each topic someone has written down."

"Let's start with you, Yosi. Can you hand me the sheet of paper you just read to the group?"

She stood up and handed me her paper.

"Great. You have a humanities degree. Can you talk about that?"

"It's like getting a degree in going to college, really," Yosi explained. "The curriculum was fairly well-rounded and taught a variety of communication, writing, and problem-solving skills through the lens of human behavior and thought. Other people in my program went on to post-secondary education, but I picked it as my major so I could get hired by people who wouldn't even consider interviewing someone who didn't go to college."

"Okay, so you can write. You can communicate effectively. And you can navigate a corporate environment," I said.

"Is there anything else around your degree that might be useful when thinking about ideas you care about?"

"Honestly," Yosi said, "college was a long time ago, and I don't think about my course of study much, other than the fact that it allowed me to get an entry-level job right out of college. I don't know if I've ever used it in the way you use some other degrees, but I suppose since I'm part of humanity, as are we all, that I do use it."

I nodded. "I get it. Let's move on. Next is grammar and spelling. Are you someone who sees typos everywhere you go?"

"Yes!" Yosi's eyes lit up. "The excess of grammatical errors in the world drives me crazy. How do other people not lose their minds?"

Jackie and Michelle chuckled, and I said, "That right there is exactly what I meant by innate talent. I'm impressed you were able to think about it in the first session, honestly."

I paused. She was giving me a meaningful look.

"Is there a typo in one of the handouts?" I asked.

She grinned. "There is. I'll show it to you later. But that's what made me think of it."

I blushed. "You're… welcome?" I replied.

"If we zoom out a level, grammar and spelling are what… proofreading?" I asked. Yogi nodded.

"Zooming out one more level, would you agree that proofreading is a subset of editing?" Again, she nodded. I looked at her. "Do you want to stop the shutter at editing, or do you want to pull back one more level, and make writing the meta category?"

She considered. "I suppose I do have thoughts about writing. I am a writer. Let's say writing."

"Your first overarching idea is writing. This is a meta category — you've already discovered some of the topics within it, and you'll find more meta categories as we continue. Let's keep going."

I picked up her piece of paper again. "Talk to me about the videos you make for your friends."

Again, her eyes lit up. "Oh! They are so fun. I take pictures and short videos when I'm with my friends and set them to music. Then, when I have enough content, I share it with them as a gift. They're so fun. They make my friends smile, and I love how even though they see me taking videos while we're together, they're always surprised when they get their gift. Disproportionately so it seems like."

"I love how excited you are about this," I said. "The way you talked just then showed how much you love this topic. It lights you up, and I can see that."

"Yeah! I saw that too," said Jackie. "It seemed like you were lit from within."

Yosi smiled. "I do really love that hobby."

"Great! Let's zoom out a level or two. Would you call it videography?"

She thought about it for a second, and said, "Yes, I think that's accurate. I shoot, I edit, I add music. That's videography."

"Make videography the meta category. Let's talk about your next bullet point. It says here that you like trying new foods and you are obsessed with your skincare routine. Those sound like different topics. Tell me about food first."

"In my town, I'm the one with her finger on the pulse of new and fun restaurants. I keep track of all the openings around town, and I have a lot of followers on Yelp. In fact, sometimes I get invited to restaurant openings and other fun things based on my Yelp reviews."

"That's a great start. It means you've already built an audience, even if you don't have any online real estate of your own. Writing about food is combining one of your existing meta categories with another. This meta category is food, which is huge," I said. "What's your skincare routine?"

"Oh, that. I have a handful of products I love." She frowned. "I know I wrote that I was obsessed with skincare but if we're pulling these back into bigger categories, skincare goes with makeup and I'm not interested in makeup or beauty in general. I've also had the same skincare routine since I was in high school, so even though I'd be happy to share it with you, I'm not seeing this as a topic that I could really dive into in greater depth."

"It's every bit as important to know the topics that don't light you up as it is to honor the ones that do. The worst thing is to try to build a business around something you really care about but don't feel like there's enough juice there. Plus, it feels like it's maybe something you want to keep for yourself."

I looked at all three women who were sitting in that room. "With people who are as smart as the three of you are, the realization Yosi had is one that will resonate with each of you. It resonates with me."

"There are so many topics I love discussing but do not want to turn into something I'm known for in business. Not all hobbies or personal interests have to be monetized."

They nodded. "Let's move on. The last category was things you can talk about for half an hour. It says here Instagram filters — that's really specific!"

Everyone laughed. Yosi was ready with a response. "Okay, maybe not just filters. But I'm really into making my Instagram pictures look like me if you know what I mean. My goal is for people to see my pictures and know I took them, without first looking at the account."

"I get that," I said. "Let's zoom out. Where does this fall under; social media or photography?"

"Hmm," Yosi said. "I don't think it's social media, the way I see it. It's more like iPhone photography. So, photography."

"Okay, we'll move on from Instagram. Now, PokemonGo? Do you want to dive more deeply into that?"

"No. That's fun, but probably because I do it with my 12-year-old nephew and we use it as an excuse to spend time together."

"What about fountain pens?" I asked.

"What about them?" Yosi said. "I have a collection of fountain pens because I love the way they write."

"I do too," I told her. "How deeply are you involved in that corner of the internet?"

She looked confused. "Fountain pens have a corner of the internet? What do you mean?"

"Oh!" I said. "That's a good point, and it highlights something I'd initially held back from mentioning since the internet can not only swallow our time but also our thinking."

"I skipped this because it almost always comes up in other ways. A board game enthusiast will likely be active on BoardGameGeek, for example. Sometimes the extra thinking time helps people remember the topics they adore."

"To your question, Yosi, yes, there's something called the Fountain Pen Network, and navigating through it is a bit like traveling back in time to when forums ran the internet, like before Reddit came in. But let's talk about social networks for a minute. Where are you most active online?"

"Do you mean anywhere other than Instagram? I'm really not active anywhere else."

I pointed to Yosi's paper, "Back to this. There's one last item on your list, Yosi, and that's hand lettering. Do you want to talk about that?"

Yosi turned to me, then looked at both Jackie and Michelle. "Hand lettering kind of peaked around the same time adult coloring books had their moment in the sun. But to me, the difference is huge. Hand lettering is basically doing calligraphy on my iPad. Other people might see it differently, but that's what it feels like to me. It's a satisfying way to spend time. It's meditative and relaxing. I find that plenty of people are afraid of it."

"Afraid of it?" I asked.

"In the sense that they think it's hard or unapproachable when in reality it's really easy. All it takes is some reason to justify buying the equipment. And it would be really fun to teach."

"Can you zoom out a level?" I asked.

"I don't think so, not with this topic. It's not the same as calligraphy, and it's not — but it is — handwriting. I think it's enough of its own category that I wouldn't feel comfortable pulling back on this one to some more general category."

"Fair enough," I said. "Can I repeat back to you the topics we found?"

Yosi nodded.

"You have editing, writing, videography, iPhone photography, and hand lettering. Does that sound like a complete list?"

"It does," Yosi said, adding, "I like how each topic is distinct and it feels like I'm the only thing connecting all five."

I smiled. "Yes! That's true. You're the through-line. Who's next?"

MINDSTORM

2

# FIND YOUR
# OVERARCHING TOPICS

So how do you do what Yosi just did? It's simple to do but harder to execute. Notice what I did: for each of the categories, I asked Yosi to dive deeper and tell me more about that. I recommend that you do just that. Put down the pen and pick up your phone and record yourself answering the question "Can you talk about that?"

Now play it back. Where do you take the conversation? In Yosi's case, and for most people, it goes in one or two directions. For her degree, the talk petered out — she was fine talking about it, but ultimately her degree and what she studied wasn't really what got her out of bed in the mornings. You could hear it explicitly and between the lines with things like "college was a long time ago."

But notice that didn't come out until I pressed a little further on her initial answer: I took the positives out of her answer (writing, communicating effectively, navigating a corporate environment) and then asked a slightly more pointed question: "Is there anything else around your degree that might be useful when thinking about ideas you care about?"

Notice I didn't tell her that these were things that she did care about — I left it open to her to say she did or she didn't. And when it came to her degree, she didn't.

But that wasn't the case with grammar and spelling. There Yosi willingly let me dial it up and broaden that interest into something bigger. And even though Yosi's degree itself was a dead end when it came to closing in on her expertise, I used what she said positively about the experience to leverage more insights here, making the connection between editing and writing, and turning writing into her first meta category.

You can see the same process at work for the discussion of her video gifts and her skincare routine. Both wound up in different places — one truly energizing her and one that just didn't get off the ground. Both outcomes are important — we're in the business of narrowing down, and if everything were a possibility then it might be hard to settle on an ultimate area of expertise.

But notice even here I wasn't trying to hit the jackpot. I want you to do the same — as you narrow down your ideas don't become enamored with one to the exclusion of the others. Find links and connections, but don't marry any of these ideas yet.

That's why I waited till I was three-quarters through her list before pivoting to "check-in" with the internet. Of course, there are many ways in which how we use it reveals things about our interests. Here are some questions to consider when exploring your different categories:

- Are you in any Facebook groups? Are you active in any of those?

- Which subreddits do you scroll through on a regular (at least weekly) basis?

- Are you part of an alternative social network? Maybe a forum or a Slack channel?

In the end, remember where Yosi landed at the end: editing, writing, videography, iPhone photography, and hand lettering. That's an amazing collection of categories that she's truly interested in, and that's where I want you to land as well.

Try the process now. If you get stuck and are looking for more inspiration, come back to the text and read either Michelle's and/or Jackie's discussion below and the techniques I used to get them to share as well. If you want help with this piece, visit MINDSTORMSbook.com and reach out.

## BOTTOM-UP AND INSIDE-OUT

Michelle handed me her paper and squared her shoulders. "I'm ready," she said.

"Let's dig into yours. I'm going to go from bottom to top instead of top to bottom like we did for Yosi, just to see what comes up. Your last bullet point says that you love your kids, of course, but you love mosaic art. I love how you wrote here that you can create something wonderful from something broken. That's such a beautiful thought. It hits me as something deep. Can you talk more about it?"

She looked like I'd caught her off guard. "I was ready to talk about what I studied in college," she said. "But this is really exciting. The art of kintsugi, or golden joinery, has been a Japanese practice for over 500 years. They take something broken — ceramic, typically — and repair it with gold, silver, or platinum. It's such a stark counterpoint to how we behave in Western culture, which is that broken things are garbage. It resonates with me, and speaks to me on a deeper philosophical level because what are we all if not deeply cracked vessels? What I do is take things that are broken, or, if my kids haven't broken anything recently, I buy things secondhand that could be broken, and I turn them into something new."

The room was silent for a moment.

"That is so lovely, Michelle," I said. "You can tell by the way we're reacting exactly how much you moved everyone. This art, these mosaics, do you give them to people as gifts, or is this a hobby you do only for yourself?"

She looked a little taken aback.

"I've never even seen them as something I could give as a gift. Simply because I don't think I could articulate their value. If I give this to someone, don't I just end up looking like a cheapskate who can't afford a real bowl or something?"

I smiled. "When you put it that way, sure. But you didn't describe it that way a moment ago. You gave this beautiful backstory and taught us something about the ancient art of making things beautiful. Don't dismiss this idea just yet. Write down "mosaics" as one of your topics." I looked at her list. "Do you want to talk about your kids?"

She hesitated, sighed, then started again. "I love making things with them, I love doing things with them, and I love being around them, but I don't see myself as a mom-blogger or a craft-with-kids person. My kids are a really important part of my life, but they aren't my life. Does that make sense?"

I nodded. "Don't push it if it doesn't work. Let's move on."

"Go into detail about some of your domestic arts. You said you don't want to build anything around your identity as a mom, but I see on your list you have creating memories, making healthy dinners that everyone will eat, and your house cleaning ideas. I'd love to learn more about those topics because I can easily think of people who have built entire empires on those pillars."

"Fair enough," she agreed. "It's funny how I differentiate making memories and being a mom. I take pictures. I like to share things that interest me with my kids and show them what it looks like to do something that lights you up. But I am not dialed into the various activities in my city that pertain to doing something with kids. So, let's skip that one, and I'll tell you a little bit about my cooking and cleaning."

She continued, after looking up. "I might be what you would call an unlikely housewife. I didn't get into my line of work, so to speak because I *just loooove* wiping snot off the faces of tiny humans or arguing incessantly about making healthy choices to someone under the age of five. I felt called to lead a house filled with children, and they fulfill me in a way that no job ever has."

"But I hate living in chaos, which is exactly what happens when you have a lot of small kids and no system. So, when my kids were small, I realized I had to do something different. I had to figure out how to feed these monsters something other than the starch and fat that humans are hardwired to love. I'm sure my kids would have loved to see how long they could go eating cheese and crackers alone, but that's not my speed. So, I figured out how to feed them vegetables and fruit in a way that reduced friction, eliminated bargaining, and filled their plates with enough nutrients that they didn't even need vitamins."

"Plus, I developed a system to make sure my house is ready for guests at any given time. I wouldn't suggest one could eat off my floors or give a white glove to check my work, but I pride myself on being able to say "yes" whenever someone wants to come over, without so much as needing to wipe down my counters."

"Now *that* is interesting," I said. "How many kids do you have?"

Michelle grinned. "Four."

"These two topics felt like they went hand in hand as you spoke, but they are distinct," I said. "House cleaning and kid-friendly vegetables. What else?"

I looked again at her list. "Do you want to discuss your course of study in college?"

She shook her head. "I'm really happy that I have a business background," she said, "because it helps me navigate ideas. Same with communication. I feel like I could easily communicate with anyone. But to talk about business or communications as a topic feels like I don't have enough background to do so. So, let's skip that."

"Okay," I said. "That just leaves the fact that you're one-half of a set of identical twins. I assume that factors into almost every aspect of your personality. Tell us about it."

"Right! It's funny, I'm 32 years old and I can count on two hands the number of things I've done — professionally or personally — that haven't included Vivian, my sister. And before you ask, I'm the older sister. By six minutes. For some reason, everyone wants to know that. But believe me, the fact that I am a twin has a lot more to do with my personality than birth order, birthstone, horoscope, Enneagram, or anything else you can chart."

"I feel like Viv is in my head. It's hard to explain to people who are sitting here not considering the thoughts and feelings of their siblings all the time. Unless you two are?" She looked at Jackie and Yosi, who shook their heads no. "Viv doesn't have the same tendencies toward entrepreneurship that I do, or at least hers are still to be discovered. So, she wasn't comfortable with my coming here. In fact, I think she's happier than I am as a stay-at-home mom. And maybe she likes the fact that until this weekend, we seemed to be on the same page with that."

"So to be here, by myself, doing something uncomfortable is heightened for me because of how utterly alone I feel. Like I should have waited for her. I should have tried to get her on the plane with me. I should have asked for another level of support. I know how it sounds. But Viv and I live in the same town. We have the same job. We both married men in the same profession. We both have the same number of kids. And even though it's a huge part of me, I do know how ridiculous it makes me sound and as such, it might not be something worth building an entrepreneurial pursuit around."

I nodded. "I understand, as much as I can, not being a twin myself. Your list is full of richness we can get into, so we can leave off being a twin, but perhaps one day you'll want to help other people in your position find their unique voice."

She visibly shuddered. "I don't see a future where that is a possibility," she said. "But okay, maybe one day. Sure."

"Thank you, Michelle," I said, then turned to address the room. "With your first ideas, it's important to focus on things you *want* to do. Finding your topics is a bit like panning for gold. You must pick up a lot of ideas and then sift through them to find the flecks you want to keep. A lot ends up getting washed away. And just like panning for gold, that's okay. You don't want sand in your ideas."

"Your list is really exciting, Michelle. I'm excited for you. Turning to Jackie I asked, "Are you ready, Jackie?"

"With Yosi, I began at the beginning and with Michelle, I started at the end. With you, I'm going to take inspiration from the poet Billy Collins. In his poem "Introduction to Poetry" he has all these lovely suggestions for how to read a poem, and your list is a little bit like a poem about your life. Two of his suggestions seem to fit you well:

I say drop a mouse into a poem
and watch him probe his way out,

or walk inside the poem's room
and feel the walls for a light switch.

I want to start in the middle as it were with what I see as your core and work our way out: you wrote here that your personality DNA is hippie, crunchy, natural, and plant-based. Why don't you take it from here?"

Jackie lit up. "Yes! It's good that you wanted to start there for me because it's through that lens that I see everything.

I haven't eaten any animals or animal products in over 13 years, and although I'm not an eat-plants proselytizer, I do want everything I do to have a positive impact on the environment and the world. I'm trying to live as plastic-free as possible, and I think about waste and our disposable culture far more often than is healthy. You can tell from my clothes and face that I live a bit differently — I haven't worn makeup since my senior prom and every piece of clothing I own has this rough-hewn organic look — but I don't want to say the word "vegan" anywhere in my materials. Online or off."

"Why's that?" I asked.

"Well, instead of answering, let me ask you: when someone tells you they're vegan, what do you expect to hear next?"

I paused, knowing she didn't need a response, not really. I waited for her to go on.

"I want to build a reputation as someone to listen to, and I know what other people think about those who lead with that word," she said. "So I won't use the word vegan. I didn't even write it on my piece of paper because it's so militant. I want to use context and nuance, not dogma and labels."

"Okay," I said. "So we have a crunchy, hippie nature. Would you call that a lifestyle?"

"Yes, I think so."

"Great. And we're leaving off the plant-based stuff for now because you don't want to write about it."

"Wait! Maybe I misspoke. I just don't want to be 'vegan Jackie' or whatever. I do think I could write and teach about how to eat more plants. Can we put that back?"

"Absolutely. So a natural lifestyle and plant-based eating. Let's go on to the next part of your list: your school background. Are you bilingual? Your paper says you double majored in English and Spanish."

She nodded. "You know how each of you talked about how your college degree only somewhat informs the direction you want to go? I will do you both one better: I grew up in a bilingual household, so I majored in the two languages I speak fluently. I didn't think much about what I wanted to study, and I'm sure I would have gone a different direction if the high school senior I once was had any ability to be introspective, but I wasn't. I cared *a lot* about getting good grades, and since I spoke Spanish at home, I knew it would be easy to double major. Honestly, my majors aren't things I think much about as an adult, with one possible exception: I am really passionate about helping my community navigate some of the more spiritual aspects of what I do."

"Helping your community navigate the more spiritual aspects of what you do," I repeated. "Can you talk a little bit more about that?"

"Sure," she said. "The energy and vibration work I do is not very well received in my community. The community I belong to is very deeply spiritual, but they tend to shy away from energy work. I want to help them demystify it and help them learn how to use the energy around them."

"Cool!" I said. "How would you categorize it? If you were to write on the tab of a folder to house your ideas around it inside, what would you write?"

"Hmm. Energy work," she replied.

"Okay. Great," I said. "That covers a lot. Does it include the Reiki like you mentioned in your yoga description?"

She nodded. "Yes, Reiki might be the right word to put on the outside of the folder because it covers a lot of energy work."

I wrote Reiki down on her list, then I went on. "What about yoga? Tell me more about what it means to you."

She looked startled as if I'd asked what breathing meant to her. "You mean other than everything? It's the reason I'm happy, mindful, centered, flexible, strong, active, and in a better mental health place than I was before I discovered yoga."

"That's a lot," I told her. "You should definitely have yoga on your list if that's what comes to mind when I ask you to tell me more." I wrote it down.

"The only thing we haven't covered is that you can talk all day long about the impact we can have on someone's day. Can you explain?"

"Oh! Sure! See, this is sort of my overarching life theme: kindness. It's why I don't eat animals; it's why I want to show my community the power of tapping into the energy of the universe. Kindness is what drives me, what moves me forward. I love seeing how a kind word, gesture, or even thought, can change my day. I like doing these little experiments. I'll walk into a coffee shop and find someone who needs a bit of positivity. Then I'll do what I can, sometimes without speaking to the person, to change their mood. It's so fun."

"That's great," I said. "You have written a beautiful phrase here: *the science behind cultivating a practice for joy.* Hold onto that. But let's make kindness your overarching word."

She nodded. "That makes sense."

# PART 2:

# FINDING YOUR IDEA

## CREATING A BODY OF WORK AS AN EXPERT

There's a lot of work that goes into Mindstorming and it can feel tiring. I get it. But there's serious payback for a morning filled with it. It may seem like you have little to show right now. But I know the full power of Mindstorming: it's like planting seeds deep beneath the surface of your consciousness, never knowing what might come up, but trusting that something will. You need to have that mindset going forward, awareness, and a willingness to plant seeds in your garden not knowing what will bloom.

That's a remarkably difficult thing for entrepreneurs to do. As a class, we all lean toward a control-based mentality. We plan. We strategize. We execute in a logical order. Randomly sprouting plants of a kind we are unprepared to tend in our garden are pretty much the exact opposite of how we imagine tending our garden.

But let me ask you: if one day an exotic, heretofore unimagined plant appeared in your garden (not a known weed), would you get rid of it, or would you do your best to discover what it might become? My experience with entrepreneurs is that they are also insatiably curious types, eager to learn new things and discover ideas that they previously didn't know. I'm betting that if you could recognize the plant for what it was — your Mindstorm — you wouldn't get rid of it but instead would tend it lovingly, making sure it got plenty of light and water.

That's what the rest of this book is about — tending those slender shoots that are the products of your Mindstorm.

By the end of the Mindstorm, you should have three to five different (in some cases *vastly different*) topics which you've discovered are your points of expertise. Write each of your overarching topics on the tab of its own manila folder or file on your computer desktop. You need a holding space for ideas related to each, and this is going to be the foundation for your entire body of work.

The point of the next part is to determine which area of expertise you are going to work with throughout the rest of the book. But since you have more than one topic, you have a bit of investigative work to do before you can move on.

# DOTS, UNDERLINES, AND ASTERISKS

Look at your list. I want you to put a dot (or @) to the left of the topic you think you're going to focus on first. Next, please underline the topic you're most passionate about and/ or like the most. Finally, I want you to put an asterisk (*) to the right of the topic you are most confident in calling yourself an expert in. You should have a dot, an underline, and an asterisk somewhere on your list.

Some of you will have all three markings converge on a single topic, in which case, you can stop here. But for most of you, the markings won't converge, which means we just need to dig deeper.

Set your folders or files aside and open a new document on your computer for this exercise (or use the worksheet provided in the workbook you can download at Mindstormsbook. com.) Start with your first topic. Write your first overarching topic at the top of the page. We're going to figure out what you think/know/feel/believe about each of your overarching topics.

You might have heard the *This I Believe* series on NPR. It's a series of audio essays by ordinary people about their core beliefs. This exercise essentially does that but narrows it down to focus on your core beliefs about your topics.

Look at the first topic you wrote down. What are your core beliefs about it? I'm asking you to think about — and write down — the ideas and opinions that when looked at individually by you probably don't seem all that special, but if you ever collected them in one place would represent an enticing overview of your entire body of knowledge around your topics.

I think you should take 15 to 20 minutes for this for your first topic to give yourself the time to really penetrate past your surface beliefs and find your core ideas. But here's what's going to happen three minutes in. After you get down a few things on my list, you're going to start to question how to frame your ideas. And that's going to make you question whether this exercise is even useful.

I know because I've done this myself several times. I was really frustrated when I attempted to articulate *my* ideas. I remember sitting down, Mindstorming alone, and writing "I don't know anything about marketing" on my sheet.

I don't want you to go there. And the way to avoid going there is to simply follow a series of prompts when jotting down everything you know. Here's the plan:

Your first prompt is **HOW** ideas: this will get you started and help you remember that you really do know a lot about your overarching topic.

Let me give you an example. If I were going to design a product to tame my curly mane, then my **HOW** ideas would include different ways to do just that. How to have great hair every day, how to dry your hair, how to apply products, how to eliminate frizz, how to love your hair again. See what I mean? You're not writing the steps on how to do it — you're just writing the idea.

Take five minutes and get your **HOW** ideas down on the page.

Now I bet if given the full 20 minutes you could build your whole body of knowledge around **HOW**. But doing that allows you to only go so deep.

The next prompt is to discover your **WHAT** ideas. What is your topic? What are the various components of your topic? Write those down for the next five minutes.

Now, the biggest ones of all: **WHY** ideas. Why is your topic important? Dive deeply into the various points of **WHY**. Go down rabbit holes here, and leave yourself space to not know exactly where you're going. These ideas, the **WHY** ideas, are the ones that will form the basis for your philosophy, so it's okay if they don't come easy (in fact, it's important that they don't come easy).

I know from my own experience that this level is hard to reach, especially when you're being timed, so give yourself ten minutes and don't be afraid of the silence at the beginning as you think out your ideas. Once you sort through your ideas, start writing down what you can in the remaining time.

I bet those last ten minutes your keyboards didn't clack as loudly as they did the first ten minutes, but I'm confident that what you put down for **WHY** was pretty good after surfacing the **HOW** and the **WHAT**.

Now, remember that this is a living document, and once we go through the next Mindstorm, you'll be able to add to it in a more robust way. Let me show you what I mean by returning to our story.

# THE FORM AND FORMAT OF AN IDEA

"Your lists of how, what, and why probably don't look like much of anything right now," I told the three women gathered around me. "You've done a great job unpacking one of those ideas, but you might feel progress is slow. And that's not a bad thing. Think of what you're doing as carving statues from marble. Your ideas might be impenetrable slabs of stone right now, but with the right tools, you'll carve your own David, just like Michelangelo."

"Here's the next exercise. Using the list that resonates with you the most, I want you now to go into deeper detail on all of your ideas -- all the **HOWS,** all the **WHATS,** all the **WHYS.** In the blogging world where I come from, this is your blog post title and meta description — a 20-word recap of what the reader can expect."

Yosi looked at me with a pained look. I could tell that the word limit was hard for her to wrap her head around — what if those 20 words weren't good enough? I knew I had to get her approaching the idea with a different mindset.

"Yosi, in your mind's eye use your most luxurious fountain pen to craft those twenty words. They don't have to be perfect, but don't hold back — let the ink bleed into the page as you write."

"Next, write **ANALOGY** in bold and tell me what this idea is like. Use something you know, not a corny sculpture analogy like I just did." Everyone smiled. "What is your idea like? How could you explain it to someone who is completely unfamiliar with your topic?"

"Analogies are truly wonderful ways to break ideas down into smaller pieces. For some people, they come naturally, and for others, they take a bit more time. I've already used photography, wine, and now sculpture as analogies and we're still on the first day. Try to think about how you would explain this topic to someone younger than you. Or someone your same age but with wholly different knowledge and expertise. There is a reason religion is taught in parables. If you can come up with an analogy, your idea will resonate more strongly."

Yosi and Michelle quickly began to type, but Jackie looked at me expectantly, a puzzled expression on her face.

I smiled and said, "Think of your idea in terms of a yoga pose." Jackie instantly smiled and started to write as well.

After a while, I piped up with the next step in the Mindstorm. "Next, write **STORY** in bold, and tell a story. Stories, like analogies, pull the reader in. There's a reason you wrote down this idea. Tell a story from your own life, or the life of someone you know. If you're telling a story from your own life, make sure it's one where you're the guide instead of the hero. Your ideas aren't about how great you are. You are great because of your ideas."

It was Michelle's turn to give me a puzzled look. She whispered, "I'm just no good at plotting a story — for some reason the whole linear thing has never worked for me."

"I would expect nothing less from someone who makes mosaic art the way you do Michelle," I replied. "Make a mosaic story, or tell it all in flashback, or use disembodied first-person voices all talking from the inside of a..." letting my voice trail off. Michelle's head was already down, and she was typing away.

After a minute I chimed in with the following: "Don't write the whole story on this doc, though. This can be a shorthand reference to something that will spark your memory when you see it."

"Next, write the phrase **OUTSIDE PROOF** on the sheet where you'll include a statistic, a data point, and/or a double-blind research study that relates to your idea. When you do this kind of research, you will find even more ideas, which can quickly lead down a rabbit hole. Take care not to read 27 Wikipedia articles about things that are not at all related to your topic. Put your computer and your brain in airplane mode if you find yourself doing this. For now, leave this part blank because finding good facts about your ideas activates a *completely different* part of your brain and is best left for a time when you're not downloading and writing out your ideas."

"You've completed your first overarching topic, one piece of your intellectual body of knowledge. Imagine how you'll feel after downloading all your ideas in this format."

Now mapping out the **HOW, WHAT,** and **WHY** is a great first step to really wrapping your hands around your idea, but it's the next Mindstorm that makes it sing.

Take your idea and describe it just like the three women did. Feel free to pretend you're writing a blog post: craft a title and a 20-word meta description of what the reader can expect.

Next, write **ANALOGY** in bold on your document, and then tell me what this idea is like. What comparison would you use to explain it to different audiences—younger audiences, older audiences, your age but with an entirely different background. What would you say to someone who is completely unfamiliar with your topic?

It's worth noting at the outset that sometimes you might get stuck doing one or more of these exercises. Recall what I did with each of the women — I went back into their topic list and pulled out an idea that really resonated with them — fountain pens, mosaic art, or yoga poses — and encouraged them to leverage their background and knowledge base in answering the question. Don't be afraid to go to your well and fish out something that will help you complete one or more of these exercises.

Next, I want you to write the **STORY** of your idea. Remember that the whole idea behind these exercises is to pull the reader in. Tell the story of your idea from your own point of view or the perspective of someone you know. And remember to keep the focus on the idea and not the narrator — this isn't a quest where they emerge as the hero — it's a chance to take the idea out for a spin and show them off.

Finally, I want you to write down the phrase **OUTSIDE PROOF**. You're not going to fill this in now because it'll take some time to do the necessary research, but I want it there as a placeholder to remind you to do the research: find the statistics, data point, or even research study to back up your idea.

I'll end with a word to the wise. Research is not flipping mindlessly from page to page on the internet. If you do that, you'll quickly find yourself way too far down a rabbit hole... and there goes your research time. Stay rigorously focused on your research and give yourself plenty of time for mental breaks (Use the Pomodoro technique when researching -- 25 minutes of research, then a five-minute break.)

Let's now hear what everyone came up with to give you a sense of what I'm hoping your idea now fleshed out sounds like.

## EVERYONE'S FIRST IDEA

After lunch, I stood in front of the group and began. "I'm excited to hear your ideas. But before we begin, I want to make something clear: this is your first idea of many. The more you download from your brain to the page, the more you'll give shape to your body of work. The point of these is to have a folder — either physical or virtual — full of your ideas that you can reach into the next time you're asked to speak or want to put together a workshop or are faced with a blank page."

I went on. "Don't get too attached to this first idea. The first idea is really the thing that will bridge the gap between where you sit now, thinking you don't have something important to say, and where you're heading, which is standing tall and comfortably in your expertise. You may not consider yourself an expert yet, but that will come."

"Now who wants to start?"

I could tell they were getting more comfortable with each other because it wasn't five seconds before Jackie volunteered.

"I'm not sure any of this is right, but I'm ready to share. The main idea is that plant-based eating is easier than you think. The meta description, is that what you call it?" looking at me with a quizzical face. I nodded. "The point is that we've come a long way since the 1970s. It's easier today than ever to follow a plant-based life. The analogy I went with for this idea was that following a plant-based lifestyle is additive, where you're focusing on the things you want to add, which makes you feel abundant, rather than focusing on the things you're taking away, which makes you feel resistance and resentment. I don't know if that's a good analogy or if it's even an analogy at all. But that's what I came up with. The story I'd tell is my personal story about becoming a plant-eater. How I felt like garbage because I was feeding my body garbage, and how spending a week at a yoga retreat that only served plant-based food made me feel a thousand times better. I'm sure there is plenty of outside proof about eating plants, but I left that blank for now."

She paused, looking at me expectantly. I could tell she was done. I paused for a second.

"That's such a great start," I said. "Most people don't get this close with their first idea. I like it. Remember, when it comes to ideas, volume is what we're going for, not perfection. You're going to want to keep picking at this one — but don't. Instead, think of all the other things you believe about this one big idea. Then map each of those using analogies, stories, and outside proof."

"Wait, that's all the feedback you have?" she asked.

"Yes, of course. Oh! You were expecting some sort of criticism? That's not going to happen here. Not today. Think of the most fragile thing you can imagine. A delicate sugar flower on a cake, let's say. And now think of how painstaking it is to build a sugar flower. I've never done it myself, but

I can imagine that it's quite a feat. It probably takes a steady hand and some tweezers to make it look right. Now let's say you've made your first one. And instead of encouragement from the sugar flower master, you got a cup of boiling water poured onto your flower. Would you want to continue with the practice of making sugar flowers?"

Every one of them shook their heads.

I nodded. "That's where we are. We're at the beginning stage, and as beginners, we are bold. We don't know how to pull ideas out 'the right way,' which means we don't know how to pull them out the wrong way. In fact, think of the format as a guide. I'm not trying to show you *the way* to go about doing things. I'm simply showing you my way. So even if you don't end up using your first topic, you've gone through the process of exploring your idea. You're not going to mess anything up by flinging your ideas onto the page. This isn't a stone tablet. It's the beginning. And that's what matters. Who's next? Yosi?"

"Sure, I'll go. I love how easy you make this. Here's my first idea: you have everything you need to start making better videos than you think. Most people let the technology — and their perception that they have the wrong kind of technology or not enough technology or not enough experience using the technology — keep them from making videos. But if you have a phone or a computer, you have enough. I was having trouble with the analogy, so the best I could come up with was that shooting videos is like riding a bike. The only way you can get better is by repetition. Do it badly, fall off, get back on. Repeat. The first story that came to mind was the story of someone I know who's a big YouTube star, but her first video was made for a friend who she really missed. She drank a bottle of wine and showed her friend how to make pasta. I don't know if this is true, but I heard that she only made the video public because she couldn't figure out how to make it private. That video went viral and she built a huge following on her drunk cooking. And all she used for that video was her phone. I didn't have a lot of data either, but just the fact that we carry around more powerful cameras and camcorders in our pockets than videographers a generation ago could afford is a big data point to me."

"Thank you, Yosi. Again, a really excellent first stab at the form and format of an idea. I love the story, too. What a fun way to accidentally go viral." I turned to Michelle and smiled. "I'm excited for your first idea."

"That makes two of us!" she exclaimed. She'd really opened up over the course of this first day. "The first idea I wrote down was why you should make cleaning your house a family activity. I feel strongly about this, and I was going to let my self-consciousness about my role as a stay-at-home mom keep me from writing this one, but I'm glad I wrote it. Because teaching your kids and your spouse and everyone who lives in your house that the best way to respect your space is to keep it clean is probably the only thing that has kept me sane. Instilling that responsibility, making everyone aware of how it's a collaborative effort and not the job of one person, is the most important life skill I can impart to my kids. It's like a puzzle, and just like a puzzle, every single piece is important. When one piece is missing, the puzzle isn't done. It's not right. It's just unfinished. You said to hold off on data, so I went straight into my story about how I always felt more stressed out at the end of my days than I did at the beginning because I used to spend an hour every morning straightening up. I'd save the vacuum and other loud things for when the kids were awake, but over time, I realized I had done everyone a huge disservice."

She looked up. "Are you familiar with that toy that comes out for the holidays? Elf on the Shelf?"

We all nodded. Jackie groaned. "Right!" Michelle replied. "It's not like parenting around the holidays isn't hard enough. That elf makes us have to do *one more thing* every night. We're supposed to move it around. Have it leave notes for the kids. It's the bane of my existence around the holidays and I fully regret ever letting it into my house. I know it sounds like I'm getting off track, but my point is that I had become, with my waking-up-early and cleaning routine, an even worse version of that darn elf."

"I was teaching my family that they were allowed to go to bed with the house in disarray and by some force of magic, they'd wake up to a clean house. That wasn't sustainable and it was making me start each day resentful."

"Ah!" I said. "I get it! Really nicely done. You've all done so well with your first ideas. That's the good news. The bad news is, you need to repeat that about a hundred more times."

## IDEA EXPLOSION

You can tell from what you heard that Yosi, Michelle, and Jackie each found a way to articulate their ideas. But let's be clear why that was the case. They were all open-minded during the Mindstorm and didn't resist delving into their ideas even if they initially might have thought them (or the exercises) corny or a waste of time. It's kind of essential that you set aside your natural (and based on past experiences perhaps even warranted) skepticism about the value of just doing a structured idea dump like this — particularly since you need to do it all again (and again) for each of your ideas on your list.

Look at your list of overarching topics. For each of them, we need to download more ideas from our brains. Following the HOW, WHAT, and WHY Mindstorm above and then the second set of exercises around the META DESCRIPTION, ANALOGY, STORY, and placeholder for OUTSIDE PROOF, I'd like you to spend 10 minutes on each idea you have listed.

Let me be clear — that's asking a lot of you. You'll need breaks to refresh your mind and clear your head between each idea. But it's worth the time and effort you'll put into each, and now that you've done one the rest will come more easily.

Here's my recommendation. Write down everything — everything you think of or believe to be true or know in your gut — about the topic you're writing about. Nothing's off-limits and there are no expectations here. Just find a way to get your thoughts down on the page because they are valid and solid.

The point of this stage is to disappear into the work. Flow is such a magical state. Somehow the ego sits aside or gets acknowledged and ignored, and beautiful words and work come out of it. It's elusive, and often doesn't happen unless you let it. Think about what helps you be your most productive and then position yourself for success by doing just that. Some of the best ideas come from people who have been out exercising all day. They come back to the page with what feels to them like an empty tank. But what comes out of their hands is something extraordinary and rare. So, find your flow state and write.

Just promise me this: when you're done and can honestly say you've fully exhausted each of your topics (or at least your favorites) you'll reward yourself for a job well done. Whether it's a session of yoga, a walk through the neighborhood, a soak in a tub, a favorite meal, or whatever else suits your fancy, give yourself a pat on the back for the work you've done today.

In fact, there's only one more thing I want you to do today. Let's listen to the final quick activity to end the day.

## ACKNOWLEDGING YOUR EXPERTISE

I wanted to keep the energy flowing, so I switched things up. On these weekends, I'd usually take the group out to dinner on the first night, but this time, my gut told me otherwise. With this combination of people and ideas, I knew staying in the nest we'd built would keep the momentum alive. So I called the restaurant, switched the reservation to tomorrow night, and ordered takeout.

When it arrived — more sushi than any four humans could reasonably expect to finish — I stood in front of everyone and resumed the programming.

"Before we eat, I want to go over the last activity of the day. It's all about acknowledging your expertise. You may think you've done enough work on your ideas today, and you have, but if you go to bed without this final exercise, you'll wake up tomorrow doubting yourselves again."

"What we're going to do is acknowledge, out loud, that we know what we're talking about. And we're going to record ourselves on video. The power of recording yourself lies in the playback. Because if we don't do this, if we leave here and go to bed, then head home, we'll be tempted to hand-wave our efforts as 'just something that happened once and can't be replicated out in the real world' where, everywhere you look, there are people who are farther along than you."

"We're planting seeds in our subconsciousness so we have some evidence to prove our inner critic wrong. This final exercise might seem superfluous, but it's not. You've done a lot of work expanding your minds today. Recording a video and standing strong in your expertise does something magical and keeps your mind open. Without it, you'll start to doubt yourselves as soon as you start to nod off tonight. But recording the video gives you proof, and since it's a different medium, it can't be as easily dismissed by your inner critic as 'just lists of words'. Who wants to start?"

Yosi stood up. "My name is Yosi, and I am an expert in editing, writing, Instagram, and hand lettering." She stopped and looked at me. "I'm not sure I can call myself an expert in all of those things."

I hit stop on the recording. "Listen," I said. "You're either trying to talk yourself out of the expertise you know you have, or something inside you is telling you not to focus on something. Do you want to try again?"

"Sure," she started. I hit the record button again. "Hi, my name is Yosi, and I'm an expert in editing, writing, and videography. That feels better. Those all feel connected. Hand lettering and Instagram are just different things. I want to lean into those three and put those other two off for at least a little while."

I stopped recording. "That's great," I said. "You can do that. I love how much more confident you sounded the second time."

I turned to Michelle. "Michelle, do you want to go next?" I hit the record button as she stood. "Hi, everyone. My name is Michelle, and I am an expert in getting your kids to do things they don't want to do — specifically house cleaning and eating vegetables. I also have some expertise in the art of mosaics, and how we can turn broken things into beautiful things."

She sounded confident, but there was still some work to be done. I kept the recording going and said, "That's a really good start. I like how you led with getting your kids to do things. I think cleaning and eating vegetables could be under one topic: parenting. I like how you described mosaics in your introduction. I thought that was great. Do you want to try it again?"

She said, "Okay, I'll try it one more time. Hi, I'm Michelle, and I'm an expert in parenting, but not in the way you think. My expertise is in getting kids to do the things that they don't think they want to do. And I get them to do things like cleaning and eating vegetables as responsible members of the household at a pretty young age. I'm also interested in the idea of turning something broken into something beautiful, and that is why I have some expertise in mosaic art."

She sat down.

"That was much better," I told her. "Jackie, we're ready."

Jackie stood up and walked confidently to the front of the room. "Hi, everyone. My name is Jackie, and I am a hippie. By that, I mean I believe in the connectedness of all things. I am an expert in all the crunchy activities you can imagine, and I eat a plant-based diet. I feel very strongly that we are all one and are all connected. And I am also an expert in reading and Reiki energy transfers."

I said, "One of the things I loved about what you said, Jackie, is that you were able to put everything under one umbrella. And as such, it's the kind of thing that will propel you moving forward. If you can stick all the ideas you came up with today into one folder, you'll show a robust body of knowledge that can help people in all sorts of ways."

Let's switch out of watching them and turn back to our own notebooks.

# YOU'RE THE EXPERT

Now it's your turn. I'm one hundred percent certain that the last thing you want to do is talk into a camera and introduce yourself and I'm one hundred percent certain that it's what you need to do to begin solidifying your view of yourself as an expert.

You're really on the cusp of blossoming here and I'd love to see that happen. So, in the immortal words of Nike, just do it. Hit record and talk into the camera, and just like Yosi, Michelle and Jackie, introduce yourself and share your expertise.

One more thing: watch the video you just recorded. If you sense any wavering at all in what you've said, don't hesitate to re-record your message. You need to end the day on a high note, not a questioning one. I want to hear you fully commit to who you are and your expertise. Don't sell yourself short, and don't end with an introduction that does either.

## IDENTIFYING THE ROOT OF THE ISSUE

I should mention that you're nowhere near done downloading ideas from your brain. In fact, here's a good spot for some more inspirational poster language around being a lifelong learner who's always coming up with more ideas. But unlike the cat poster I posted early on, I really do mean this.

Let me be completely transparent about what I mean. I've personally written out over 200 ideas in this format, and I'm *still* writing them. They're the foundation for everything I do, and because *I make time to create them* when I'm thinking about what I want to put together next, I never have to start from scratch.

So find your lines in the sand. Your soapboxes. The unpopular ideas that show a different angle. Because what you're looking for, what you want to uncover through this work, is a problem that can be solved through your ideas and your thought leadership.

What do I mean by a problem? Well, whether you think of your ideas as a solution to a problem or not, that's what they are. And that's a good thing. Why? Because people are willing to pay to solve problems.

So when you're looking at your ideas, think about the problem that they solve. The problem should be *intense* for someone because otherwise why would they want to solve it? The problem should also be something that a person can't solve on their own, so it can't be trivial. If you have a nail and a hammer, you don't have a problem — at least not for long. It's going to be hard, if not impossible, for you to get much traction solving hammer and nail problems.

But most of all, the best problems should also uncover a deeper fear. It's not enough for you to state a problem they know they have and they want to solve. What is the root of the problem? Put another way, what's the real issue? That is often where you can really connect with people.

The last piece is up to you. How do you, the expert, see the problem? If you can state the problem in your own words and show people how they can solve it, with you, you've set yourself up for success.

So here's my recommendation: while you're developing your ideas and downloading your knowledge, come up with a list of problems that you can solve. Because again, you could solve a problem by writing a book, you could solve a problem by speaking on the stage, you could solve a problem by facilitating a workshop or coaching somebody one on one. The delivery methods are the least important. Figuring out the problems you solve is the first step toward figuring out which delivery method you'll use first.

You can see what I mean by listening in on the conversation I had with the three women after dinner.

After clearing away the dishes and pouring another glass of wine, I turned and said "Let's do a final brain download for the evening. I'll set the timer for ten minutes, and you write down one problem that you solve. That's your main topic. But along the way I want you to identify the real underlying problem that's driving the issue. Finally, write your ideas on how to solve it, and therefore solve the surface problem."

After time was up I turned to the group and said, "Let's discuss your thoughts."

"I'll go first," Michelle said. "The topics I came up with today were mosaics, house cleaning, and getting kids to eat vegetables. I wasn't sure which one I wanted to start with, but the one that kept coming up when I thought about problems I could solve was housecleaning. The problem is how to keep the house clean when you have four kids without going crazy. That's the big problem. But the underlying problem is shame. People are afraid to have people drop by, or give limited notice and come see your house when it's not in shape for company. I can teach people how to have a house that's always clean enough for a friend or family member to stop by. The way I see it, the time you are spending cleaning frantically could be spent doing all kinds of other things. And that's what I'm hoping to show."

"I already want that, and I don't have any kids!" Yosi said.

"Same here," said Jackie. "I'd love to have people over on a whim. That aligns with my personality. But keeping a house clean is hard."

I said, "See? Off the top of your head, you were able to articulate your expertise and the problems you can solve in such a way that everyone at the table wanted to learn more. I love how you talked about time — using it mindfully instead of wasting it — because that aligns with your adjacent interests. The people who would be interested in your ideas around keeping a house clean are the same people who are making time for healthy dinners with their kids. They are parents who want to spend their time making memories with their kids instead of forcing them to eat their vegetables. You're offering peace of mind and releasing people from the shame of not having a clean house. That is a magnificent place to start."

I turned to Yosi. "Do you want to go next?"

"Sure. I need a bit more help than Michelle, and I'm trying not to be envious of how easily that came out for her," Yosi replied. "I am a writer, an editor, and a videographer. So my initial thought was to hang up a shingle and offer those services to people who want them. Am I thinking about it wrong? Should I instead teach people how to do that for themselves?"

I nodded. "I'm glad you brought that up because it's something I struggled with too. My background is in providing marketing services. Not only can I tell someone how to market themselves, but I can also implement marketing strategies for people, and I can do it faster than they can do it themselves. In fact, when I first started coaching, I kept changing the contracts partway through the engagement. I'd get hired to coach someone through building profitable marketing engines, then swap out a session or two for a website redesign. So to say I understand your hesitation is putting it mildly. It took a long time for me to get comfortable with the role of coach, which is *far different from* the role of service provider. So let me turn the question back on you. Take editing, for example. Let's say you could earn $10,000 per month editing. How much time would you guess you'd be spending on editing?"

She shrugged. "I expect it would be pretty close to full-time if I were to get to that level doing editing. I don't know that I could charge enough to make more than that doing straight editing work."

"Exactly," I said. "That's exactly the problem. You might think I picked editing because I knew it had a low ceiling. But let's take videography. Maybe you can do videography on less than a full-time basis and get to $10,000 per month, but how could you get to $60,000 per month on that?"

She chuckled. "You move to Hollywood and get your big break."

I smiled. "Fair enough, but let's assume not everyone wants to do that. My point is that services are hard to scale. Not impossible, but hard. Let's go back to editing. What problem do people have that a great editor can solve?"

"They're writing online, and their writing isn't polished," Yosi said.

"Can you help people figure out how to edit their own stuff?" I asked.

"I think I could. I have this method that I go through when I'm editing something. I go through a piece of writing six times, looking for something different each time."

"Excellent, let's explore that. Your method needs a name. Something like the six-pass edit method. Once you have a name and a promise, you have something that solves a problem for people. Because you could teach all six passes, no problem."

"Interesting," Yosi said. "I like that."

"It's a good start. Jackie? What are some problems that you solve?"

Jackie took a sip of her tea. "People want to eat more plants. They keep hearing that it's good for the Earth and good for their bodies. But they don't know *how* to do it. And it's not as simple as telling someone to simply eat more vegetables because that's not helpful. They know they should eat more vegetables, but their wiring is such that vegetables are seen as punishment. And vegetables don't have to be punishment! They want to figure out a way to change their habits for good."

She turned to Michelle. "Michelle, it's funny, the things I'm thinking about are some of the same things you're thinking about."

Michelle smiled. "You're right. Getting kids to eat vegetables is not all that different than getting adults to eat vegetables."

"Right! The people I want to help are those who are trying to be kinder to themselves and the planet. But they don't know how to get started. So the big problem I'd like to solve is learning how to add more plants without giving up your whole life. I think the underlying problem I face is resistance to change and fear that they'll never get to eat their favorite treat ever again. I'd like to guide people toward adding plants without demonizing treats and favorite indulgences in the process."

I paused. "I think that's great. In fact, I think each one of you has an idea that can take you to $10,000 months. But I bet I can guess your next question: where should you start? Of all the methods I quickly listed, the first one each of you should start with is coaching. You might be thinking that each of these problems could be solved through an online course, and we'll get into those tomorrow because you're right. Courses are a great way to scale. But coaching is the way to get paid to develop that content."

"Think of it this way: Jackie, you could call yourself a mindful plant coach. Yosi, you could coach people through the six-pass method of editing your own writing. Michelle, you can coach people through the steps you go through to keep your house clean enough for spontaneous guests. You have all these ideas and all these methodologies."

"You can start charging between $2500 and $5000 for six to 12 one-hour coaching sessions. Then those sessions become the framework for your digital course. And that's how you can scale that kind of thing without having to build more things or figure out how to get a higher-paying service job. Does that make sense?"

They all nodded.

I stood. "I'm going to let you sit with this. Enjoy the rest of the wine — there's more in the fridge — and we'll come back tomorrow to talk about where we're going from here. You're off the hook for today! I'll see you in the morning."

MINDSTORM

6

# SOLVING PROBLEMS

I should mention that you're nowhere near done downloading ideas from your brain. In fact, here's a good spot for some more inspirational poster language around being a lifelong learner who's always coming up with more ideas. But unlike the cat poster I posted early on, I really do mean this.

Let me be completely transparent about what I mean. I've personally written out over 200 ideas in this format, and I'm still writing them. They're the foundation for everything I do, and because I make time to create them when I'm thinking about what I want to put together next, I never have to start from scratch.

So find your lines in the sand. Your soapboxes. The unpopular ideas that show a different angle. Because what you're looking for, what you want to uncover through this work, is a problem that can be solved through your ideas and your thought leadership.

What do I mean by a problem? Well, whether you think of your ideas as a solution to a problem or not, that's what they are. And that's a good thing. Why? Because people are willing to pay to solve problems.

So when you're looking at your ideas, think about the problem that they solve. The problem should be intense for someone because otherwise why would they want to solve it? The problem should also be something that a person can't solve on their own, so it can't be trivial. If you have a nail and a hammer, you don't have a problem — at least not for long. It's going to be hard, if not impossible, for you to get much traction solving hammer and nail problems.

But most of all, the best problems should also uncover a deeper fear. It's not enough for you to state a problem they know they have and they want to solve. What is the root of the problem? Put another way, what's the real issue? That is often where you can really connect with people.

The last piece is up to you. How do you, the expert, see the problem? If you can state the problem in your own words and show people how they can solve it, with you, you've set yourself up for success.

So here's my recommendation: while you're developing your ideas and downloading your knowledge, come up with a list of problems that you can solve. Because again, you could solve a problem by writing a book, you could solve a problem by speaking on the stage, you could solve a problem by facilitating a workshop or coaching somebody one on one. The delivery methods are the least important. Figuring out the problems you solve is the first step toward figuring out which delivery method you'll use first.

You can see what I mean by listening in on the conversation I had with the three women after dinner.

After clearing away the dishes and pouring another glass of wine, I turned and said "Let's do a final brain download for the evening. I'll set the timer for ten minutes, and you write down one problem that you solve. That's your main topic. But along the way I want you to identify the real underlying problem that's driving the issue. Finally, write your ideas on how to solve it, and therefore solve the surface problem."

After time was up I turned to the group and said, "Let's discuss your thoughts."

"I'll go first," Michelle said. "The topics I came up with today were mosaics, house cleaning, and getting kids to eat vegetables. I wasn't sure which one I wanted to start with, but the one that kept coming up when I thought about problems I could solve was housecleaning. The problem is how to keep the house clean when you have four kids without going crazy. That's the big problem. But the underlying problem is shame. People are afraid to have people drop by, or give limited notice and come see your house when it's not in shape for company. I can teach people how to have a house that's always clean enough for a friend or family member to stop by. The way I see it, the time you are spending cleaning frantically could be spent doing all kinds of other things. And that's what I'm hoping to show."

"I already want that, and I don't have any kids!" Yosi said.

"Same here," said Jackie. "I'd love to have people over on a whim. That aligns with my personality. But keeping a house clean is hard."

I said, "See? Off the top of your head, you were able to articulate your expertise and the problems you can solve in such a way that everyone at the table wanted to learn more. I love how you talked about time — using it mindfully instead of wasting it — because that aligns with your adjacent interests. The people who would be interested in your ideas around keeping a house clean are the same people who are making time for healthy dinners with their kids. They are parents who want to spend their time making memories with their kids instead of forcing them to eat their vegetables. You're offering peace of mind and releasing people from the shame of not having a clean house. That is a magnificent place to start."

I turned to Yosi. "Do you want to go next?"

"Sure. I need a bit more help than Michelle, and I'm trying not to be envious of how easily that came out for her," Yosi replied. "I am a writer, an editor, and a videographer. So my initial thought was to hang up a shingle and offer those services to people who want them. Am I thinking about it wrong? Should I instead teach people how to do that for themselves?"

I nodded. "I'm glad you brought that up because it's something I struggled with too. My background is in providing marketing services. Not only can I tell someone how to market themselves, but I can also implement marketing strategies for people, and I can do it faster than they can do it themselves. In fact, when I first started coaching, I kept changing the contracts partway through the engagement. I'd get hired to coach someone through building profitable marketing engines, then swap out a session or two for a website redesign. So to say I understand your hesitation is putting it mildly. It took a long time for me to get comfortable with the role of coach, which is far different from the role of service provider. So let me turn the question back on you. Take editing, for example. Let's say you could earn $10,000 per month editing. How much time would you guess you'd be spending on editing?"

She shrugged. "I expect it would be pretty close to full-time if I were to get to that level doing editing. I don't know that I could charge enough to make more than that doing straight editing work."

"Exactly," I said. "That's exactly the problem. You might think I picked editing because I knew it had a low ceiling. But let's take videography. Maybe you can do videography on less than a full-time basis and get to $10,000 per month, but how could you get to $60,000 per month on that?"

She chuckled. "You move to Hollywood and get your big break."

I smiled. "Fair enough, but let's assume not everyone wants to do that. My point is that services are hard to scale. Not impossible, but hard. Let's go back to editing. What problem do people have that a great editor can solve?"

"They're writing online, and their writing isn't polished," Yosi said.

"Can you help people figure out how to edit their own stuff?" I asked.

"I think I could. I have this method that I go through when I'm editing something. I go through a piece of writing six times, looking for something different each time."

"Excellent, let's explore that. Your method needs a name. Something like the six-pass edit method. Once you have a name and a promise, you have something that solves a problem for people. Because you could teach all six passes, no problem."

"Interesting," Yosi said. "I like that."

"It's a good start. Jackie? What are some problems that you solve?"

Jackie took a sip of her tea. "People want to eat more plants. They keep hearing that it's good for the Earth and good for their bodies. But they don't know how to do it. And it's not as simple as telling someone to simply eat more vegetables because that's not helpful. They know they should eat more vegetables, but their wiring is such that vegetables are seen as punishment. And vegetables don't have to be punishment! They want to figure out a way to change their habits for good."

She turned to Michelle. "Michelle, it's funny, the things I'm thinking about are some of the same things you're thinking about."

Michelle smiled. "You're right. Getting kids to eat vegetables is not all that different than getting adults to eat vegetables."

"Right! The people I want to help are those who are trying to be kinder to themselves and the planet. But they don't know how to get started. So the big problem I'd like to solve is learning how to add more plants without giving up your whole life. I think the underlying problem I face is resistance to change and fear that they'll never get to eat their favorite treat ever again. I'd like to guide people toward adding plants without demonizing treats and favorite indulgences in the process."

I paused. "I think that's great. In fact, I think each one of you has an idea that can take you to $10,000 months. But I bet I can guess your next question: where should you start?

Of all the methods I quickly listed, the first one each of you should start with is coaching. You might be thinking that each of these problems could be solved through an online course, and we'll get into those tomorrow because you're right. Courses are a great way to scale. But coaching is the way to get paid to develop that content."

"Think of it this way: Jackie, you could call yourself a mindful plant coach. Yosi, you could coach people through the six-pass method of editing your own writing. Michelle, you can coach people through the steps you go through to keep your house clean enough for spontaneous guests. You have all these ideas and all these methodologies."

"You can start charging between $2500 and $5000 for six to 12 one-hour coaching sessions. Then those sessions become the framework for your digital course. And that's how you can scale that kind of thing without having to build more things or figure out how to get a higher-paying service job. Does that make sense?"

They all nodded.

I stood. "I'm going to let you sit with this. Enjoy the rest of the wine — there's more in the fridge — and we'll come back tomorrow to talk about where we're going from here. You're off the hook for today! I'll see you in the morning."

# PART 3:

# POSITIONING YOUR BRAIN

MINDSTORM

7

# POSITIONING THE EXPERT

In Part 3 we are going to firm up your belief in your expertise and give yourself permission to dream a little bit bigger.

But before we do that you need to introduce yourself to yourself again. I want you to get comfortable such that you can hear your voice clearly joining this chorus:

"I'm Kathleen and I'm an expert in seeing business opportunities and ideas in businesses that don't even exist yet."

"I'm Jackie and I'm an expert in kindness."

"I'm Michelle, and I'm an expert in homemaking."

"I'm Yosi and my expertise is in creativity through videography."

And now it's your turn to introduce yourself. Find Mindstorm 7 in the workbook. It's a quick one.

Let me be clear: expertise is a solid foundation, but expertise alone is not enough. The smartest person in the room is very rarely the one who has become the most successful, or even the happiest. It's a sad fact, but it's the truth. For each of the folders that you, and Yosi, Michelle, and Jackie, have developed — like kindness, homemaking, and creative expression — there are hundreds if not thousands of other people doing the exact same thing.

Now, on the one hand, I can imagine that hearing that is discouraging. But in fact, it's good to know that you don't have to uncover a new element, discover a star in the outer realms of the universe, or figure out the cure to the common cold in order to be successful. Other people are doing it because there's a real need that you can meet. What we're going to work on in this part is the kind of work you're going to do to start getting known in your respective spaces.

# DREAM A LITTLE DREAM

Here's how we're going to begin. As is the custom in my weekend retreats, we're going to begin... with a daydream. Here's how it worked with the three women on the retreat.

"We're daydreaming, and in this daydream, we're going to fast forward five, maybe ten years. Close your eyes. What do you see? You've done some pretty remarkable things in your field. What is that like? Can you see it? I'm going to pause here and let you visualize your future self. This is a remarkably powerful exercise because unlike a business plan with spreadsheets and formulas and all that right-brained 'important' stuff, it's allowing you to see yourself through a new lens. Think of where you are as a spot on a map. The road unwinds in front of you, and the path diverges. You don't have to be Robert Frost to see that these paths don't have the same destination. One goes left, one goes right.

Your life, as it exists if you hadn't come to this retreat, is the path on the left. And the one from the daydream is the path on the right. Where does it lead? I'm going to give you ten minutes to write about this new path."

(Let me just state the obvious at this point: if they are doing it, you should be doing it. Set the timer and write!)

They wrote and wrote. I gave them a two-minute warning. They kept going, right up to the ten-minute mark.

"What you've written there is raw. It's not for sharing. It's not even for reading, not right now. I want you to acknowledge the resistance that came up when you wrote. The what-ifs and what-abouts and did-you-considers that always come up when you take a creative leap."

"Now it's easy to ask what would it take to make your day-dream a reality, but I want to offer some concrete steps in that direction. Because if you read that Robert Frost poem closely you see he says that "knowing how way leads on to way / I doubted I should ever come back." One way to ensure that you reach your destination is to take that road, and I want to start you down that path today."

"How can you do that?" I asked. "Well, we started with expertise because understanding you're an expert leads to a far better understanding of what it takes to position yourself as the expert that you are. Because without the expertise we established, you'll start second-guessing yourself with the next thing I'm going to tell you. Step one was establishing your expertise, step two is positioning yourself as the expert, and entering into the market at a higher level."

"There are two ways to position yourself as an expert. These two tips are *so good* that they'll feel like shortcuts or hacks because of how quickly they can elevate you. Ready?"

"Write a book and speak on a stage."

MINDSTORM

9

# WRITE A BOOK

Before you scoff and say that you're not the kind of person who writes books, ask yourself this: six months ago, were you the kind of person who would seriously engage with a book like this and do the kind of Mindstorming we've been doing?

So hear me out: you may not want to write a book. You may not even think you know *how* to write a book. Or what would go in your book. You may not think you have enough experience to write a book. To that, I say, you're right. But you have all the knowledge you need. And the absolute best way to enter the market at a higher level is to have a published book with your name on it.

When I tell this to clients like Yosi, Michelle and Jackie I can tell they don't dismiss it right out of hand. People like them — people like you — take seriously what it would mean to take on what seems like a herculean task.

So let me say something shocking: writing a book is easier than you think. It comes down to two things:

One is getting inspired by all the books out there, and thinking to yourself if they can do it, what's stopping me?

Two is surrounding yourself with other people who are working toward the same goal.

Because the old saying is true: when someone says, 'so-and-so wrote the book on it' what they're trying to tell you is that so-and-so really knows what they're talking about. And that so-and-so could be you.

Let's also be clear: business books do not have to rival *War and Peace* in terms of length. The book you hold in your hands was not written to compete with Tolstoy or Dickens or any other 19th-century novelist. My friend Erin Donley is a nonfiction author and a consultant for other nonfiction writers, and her goal is to get more so-called "airplane reads" out into the world. Her main point is that if you can't read a business book in the span of an airplane flight, it's too long.

The upside of having written a book is huge. Once you've published your book, the media becomes much more interested in what you have to say. It'll be easier to talk about things on your local television station as well as any podcast. People want to talk to people who have expertise, and you demonstrate yours more effectively if you have a book. It's amazing what having a published book can do for you in terms of elevating your status in the eyes of your audience. It is much easier than it would be without a platform at all.

The truly amazing thing about where all you are right at this very moment is that you've just minted your ideas. They're fresh, which means you're not coming to the task of writing a book with any sort of established platform or posting schedule or anything that would prevent you from doing the work to getting a book written.

Here's a final way you can make writing your first book easier. I think you should commit right now to writing ten books over the course of the rest of your life.

I know it sounds crazy, but hear me out. Deciding to write ten books makes the mountain of the idea of writing one book into a much smaller hill — a hike if you will. And it takes the pressure off because your first book isn't the only one you'll ever write, which means it doesn't have to be any sort of Magnum Opus. It's simply the first of a series of books you're going to write, which means your first one doesn't have to have *absolutely everything you know* in it. In a sense, committing to writing a shelf of books takes the pressure off of a person who's trying to make their first book Something Important That People Need.

And don't worry about getting published. Even though we're going to publish many books in our lifetimes, we aren't going to wait for book deals. We're authors and speakers, mentors and coaches, workshop facilitators and consultants. So that's why we're going to self-publish. Getting a book written is one of those instant credibility things that little else offers. And once you write your first one, you'll know what the process looks like, and you'll be able to publish your next one in less time.

So here's what you should do. Commit to writing your first book. Then, take your mind downloads, and see how they could be organized in your book. Congratulations! You have an outline!

When I tell groups I'm facilitating that they need to publish a book I usually can talk them around to my point of view. But when I say they need to make a speech is when I really run into major resistance. Just look and see what happened with Yosi, Michelle, and Jackie.

MINDSTORM

# 10

# SPEAK ON A STAGE

"The other shortcut to a higher platform is to deliver an amazing speech. This suggestion makes people who hate public speaking cringe, or worse, look for the way out. But again, it's not as big of a thing as it seems."

I immediately got a round of skeptical looks from all three women. By the looks on their faces, I might have well suggested howling at the moon as a business strategy. But I pressed on.

"In fact, this is something you can do *well before* you have your first book written. And you can do it from the comfort of your home. All you need is your idea, a slide deck, and an internet connection, and you can present in front of people from all over the world. This is something I do with my clients who are trying to sell their offers (often digital products or services) to people without having to be in the same room they are."

"One of the best places to get inspired is by watching Ted talks. My friend Terri Trespicio has an amazing one titled 'Stop Searching for Your Passion.' You can find it on YouTube. It's gotten millions of views, but yours doesn't have to in order to change your life. Consider this: if you were to give a talk about a very specific part of the ideas you've already downloaded, what would it be?"

"I don't mean to get us off track," said Michelle, "but setting aside the fact that I would be mortified at doing what you describe, how does giving a speech even help us build a business? Isn't that what this weekend was supposed to be about? Tapping into our inner entrepreneur? It seems like coming up with a keynote speech or even writing a book is just … irrelevant."

Yosi and Jackie nodded. "Yeah! I thought today would be about making money," Yosi said.

"You're right," I said, smiling. "Today is about figuring out how to position yourself to make money on your knowledge. I like to plant two seeds that, once they take root, will increase your success in ways you can't imagine right now. They're surprisingly simple — not easy, none of this is easy — shortcuts to making more money. But you're absolutely right — speaking on a stage or self-publishing a book will get you some attention, but neither one of those activities will earn you money right away."

"I'm giving you advice I wish I'd followed myself. If someone told me to write a book a year when I was starting out — *and if I'd listened to them* — I'd have a lot more to show for myself, which makes me suggest writing your first book right off the bat. I have a friend who has built a very lucrative business for herself on the back of a TedX talk that went viral. So I know these two things help you build enough confidence to charge more for your expertise. But that's my experience coloring this. So let's take a step back."

# MAP OUT YOUR
# COACHING PROGRAM

I really meant what I said to those women and what I'm saying to you now. Writing a book and giving a talk are two simple ways to gain credibility that will position you to make more money. To see why let's switch gears for a second to talk about <u>how</u> you'll make money. There's one way to start earning income on your experience right away, and that's to set yourself up as a coach.

To be clear, I define being a coach a bit differently than other people. When I say coach, I mean that you'll take your topic and help people, one on one, solve a problem through the idea you mapped out in previous Mindstorms.

You need to answer the same questions I asked the women at the Mindshop. If someone approached Yosi and wanted to learn about videography, how could she help them? Or if a parent reached out to Michelle and wanted to know how to change the way their home works even with young kids? Or what would Jackie say to someone with health issues who's curious about plant-based eating?

Right now I firmly believe you know enough about your topics of expertise that you could map out six coaching sessions. Why six? It's a good number for coaching sessions. You can get a lot solved by meeting someone every week for six weeks or every other week for three months.

Now ask yourself what would each of those sessions cover? Work from the end. What will that person get once they're done working with you? Now, break up each piece of that eventual outcome and assign it to one of the six sessions. Take 20 to 30 minutes right now and allow yourself to create the framework of a one-on-one coaching program — a coaching Mindstorm if you will. Don't be shy — just dig in.

When you are finished and can see the path to the outcome, I want you to answer just one more question for yourself: if someone went through your six sessions, would they come out transformed?

I think your answer should be yes. In fact, I'm betting that it is. Certainly whoever hired you for coaching is doing so because they don't have your expertise. And after being coached by you they come away vastly more knowledgeable, which means only one thing:

You should be charging a lot for each of these sessions. Start with $5,000 for six sessions.

I know what you're thinking. You're thinking that you can't. Worse, you're thinking that you shouldn't.

But remember this: there are people out there who aren't as good as you are who are charging premium rates. Keep in mind that when you're changing someone's life, you need to charge them enough so they're incentivized to take action. If you charge someone too little for six sessions, they're far less likely to show up for your sessions, let alone put in the hard work than they would if you charged them enough for them to feel it in their bank account.

But let's table the money discussion for the moment because I want to talk about the real genius of delivering coaching. Because once you deliver your knowledge to one person at a time and capture their transformation, you can use that to help you build your digital products. That did not take long at all to show Yosi, Michelle, and Jackie.

# BRAINSTORM YOUR DIGITAL PRODUCTS

"If you coach someone, you've essentially done all the work to create a roadmap for anything that comes after, and can scale, and — bonus — you've taken it for a test drive. That's why I'm advising you to strongly consider offering yourself as a coach. The way to wealth is by positioning yourself as the expert. I've seen people hesitate at this stage, to their detriment. They think they need to build their expertise by creating a complex digital product, but the truth is, coaching or mentoring someone one on one means you only need to convince yourself that you can teach one person, which is easier to do."

"If you're tempted by creating digital products as a way to avoid coaching, ask yourself how much stronger they might be if they logically flowed out from that process instead of being created whole cloth out of thin air."

I looked up. "I know it seems like I'm repeating myself, but this is something I wish I'd done at the onset, so I'm hoping you'll avoid that same fate. Let's move onto digital products."

"Digital products — courses, template bundles, outlines, kits — are a great way to start making money. It might feel too soon to think about building a product since the ink on your expertise hasn't had time to dry, but one of the beautiful things about Mindstorming is that we're traveling to a different world. When I'm Mindstorming, I picture myself up in the clouds, floating. I'm weightless, and since I'm defying the laws of gravity, defying other more ho-hum laws like the laws of limitations imposed on myself, by myself, is easier. The walls just fade away."

"The walls we're looking to dismantle are the ones I call 'but-how's.' Your job, as Mindstormer-in-chief, is *not* to figure out how to do any of the things you dream up. Remember, you can float and fly. Figuring out how to implement something is something your future self can take care of. Right now I just want you to come up with the ideas. Deal?"

"Deal," they all said in unison.

Let's get clear on the problem you are solving and who you are solving it for. Now plenty of ink has been spilled discussing client avatars, but that's overcomplicating something that's more simple. Because once you're clear on the problem you're solving, all you have to do is decide who you're solving it for.

MINDSTORM

13

# BUILD YOUR NETWORK

Brainstorm 100-150 people who know you and value you. Go beyond your friends and family and use your social networks to find your connections. Your Facebook friends and LinkedIn connections are a good place to start. They know who you are professionally. Find them and talk to them. Let them know what you're up to, and ask if they know anyone who has the problem you solve.

Make sure you're involving your community as you're building your knowledge business. Let them help you. Remember that people want to help you, especially if they like you. And they *will* like you. So let them. Ask for help. Ask for what you need. See if anyone can get you on a stage — either virtual or physical — and see if they have connections to publications.

You know that old adage, it's not what you know, it's who you know? I'd like to challenge you to take that a step further. It's not really who you know, it's who knows you. You'll find that there are plenty of people in your circles who are *really connected*. And because you're who you are, there will always be people who want to help you. So find those people.

I have a friend who collects experts as if she has an old Rolodex. Every time someone comes to her asking if she knows anyone who can speak about something, she finds people and elevates them. There are people in your life who will do that for you. This isn't a case where you look for people like you're a predator seeking prey. Find friends. Align yourself with others who are doing the same thing. Help everyone succeed.

If you have 100-150 conversations with people who already know, like, and trust you, and you are open and vulnerable about conveying your expertise, you will learn so much from the conversations you have about what you should build based on the ideas you've downloaded, and chances are, you'll have your first several clients from that as well.

MINDSTORM
14

# PUT A NUMBER ON IT

Positioning differentiates you from everyone else. Make sure you know your value and that the people who know you know what you offer.

When it comes to positioning, it's time for big expansive thinking. Start small, invest wisely, but think big. Keep your eye on your destination, but make sure your focus and activity are appropriate to where you are.

And how do you do that you ask? Listen to the advice I gave to Yosi, Michelle, and Jackie.

"Sometimes I'm asked how to think big. Let's start from the end and work backward. Step one: write the dollar amount you'd like to earn from your ideas."

I looked at Yosi, then Michelle, and finally Jackie. No one moved. Not a single keystroke was heard, nor a single pen scratched the page.

I smiled. "You're going to make me channel my inner Dr. Evil from Austin Powers and say, *ONE MILLION DOLLARS*, aren't you?" I asked while moving my pinky to my mouth. That at least elicited a smile from the group.

"I like to ask this question without any context just to see where people land, but since you're staring at me like there's something in my teeth it's probably wise for me to explain myself. When I've asked the revenue question without context, most people answer in terms they understand, an annual income. It's typically six figures, often in the low six figures. So instead of thinking about annual salary, focus on monthly income. It's easier to work toward earning ten thousand dollars in a month than it is to work toward a hundred and twenty thousand dollars in a year."

"Why?" Yosi asked.

I nodded. "Good question. It's the same reason we put 23 things on a to-do list versus one massive item: humans are good at small, manageable tasks, which is what earning $10,000 in one month is, but not great at huge tasks that seem impossible. If something feels impossible to you, your brain will ensure that it stays outside the realm of possibility for you."

"And if you fail to take things one month at a time, you'll find yourself hitting lower income ceilings because you won't push yourself. After you've earned $10,000 in a month, chances are, you'll be able to see the path toward $20,000. But it's significantly more challenging to visualize doubling your annual income. It's impossible to imagine, sitting here, that in a few years you'll earn $720,000 in one twelve-month period, but it isn't so hard to think you'll get to connect a series of $60,000 months on your own intellectual property."

I want to jump in here and interrupt the narrative to just share one thought directly. There are three ways you can think about value that will help you put a number on it.

Number one is to value your expertise. Put yourself in the shoes of your client to remind yourself of the value you provide. Consider the surgeon. That person has trained for a very long time to make their job look easy. So have you. You've trained for this.

Number two is to value your time. Let's say you've set your mid-term goal to $20,000 per month. That means you're selling and delivering $5,000 per week. That makes your time worth $1000 per workday. If your time is worth $1000 per day, you have to stop doing $35 per hour tasks.

And number three is to value *their* time. Your clients do not want to spend as much time as you did developing their expertise. They want the shortcuts. They want to learn from your mistakes. So do not pad your delivery. You don't need something to be heavy or take a long time to be valuable.

Now back to our regularly scheduled programming…

"Maybe it's the scenery," Yosi said, breaking the silence after what felt like forever, but was probably only five or six minutes, "but what I'm filled with is this distinct possibility that not only is building a life where I'm making good money from my ideas doable, but it's doable *for me*. I didn't think I'd get to this point mentally so quickly, but I'm happy I came." She turned to me, and I looked back.

"I almost didn't come," she said in a confidential tone. I could tell this was something of a heavy load that she wanted to unburden.

"I'm glad you were able to get here," I said.

"You know, it's funny," she said, after a pause, "I haven't ever done anything like this before. Nothing for myself. I've never even gotten a massage. I don't buy into self-care, I don't feel like I should have time for myself. I know where it comes from, but somehow it felt really indulgent to come to this… I still have to remind myself that it's a Mindshop."

"Me too!" Michelle jumped in. "I mean, who am I to take three days to do something I want to do?"

"Right?" Yosi said. "But the thing I am realizing now that we're partway through our second day together is that this retreat is showing me some possibilities I didn't know existed. And the most surprising thing I'm finding is how little resistance I'm feeling about these different income levels. Maybe that's because we're talking about precious metals, but not once in this morning session have I felt like any of this was unreachable for me."

"Yes! That's exactly it!" Michelle exclaimed. "And I think that shift, from this being an indulgent waste of time to being the thing that plants the seeds for what will become my new life. The biggest surprise for me has been how little resistance I'm having to listening to the income possibilities. The way it's laid out feels natural, like a progression I can see."

"That is interesting," I said. "Because this retreat isn't about self-care or relaxation. For a lot of people, these retreats represent the most work they've done on their own business in one weekend."

"This is by far the most work I've done downloading ideas from my brain," Jackie said. "But if I step back, and try to math this out, I find my resistance coming back up. "I can't make $240,000 with the hippie crap I know!" is what the voice says. But then we get right back into it and I'm sitting here taking notes and thinking, okay sure, I'll be sure to watch out for that once I get to the next money stage."

"That is precisely what's so powerful about this imagery," I said, "and it's what I want you to come back to when you find yourself feeling resistance. Don't do year-long math, just plan for your next month."

# 90-DAY EXPERIMENTS

Let's say you're not sure whether you want to start monetizing your ideas through coaching. You've read the last section, you understand the power of teaching someone one on one, you've brainstormed your six sessions.

Do yourself a favor and give it 90 days. Decide, right now, that you'll position yourself as a coach — at least through the next Mindshops — and build everything you need to do that. Then test it out for the next 90 days.

You can find out very quickly in 90 days where it is headed for the short and medium-term. And that means that you can test your ideas in real-time.

Here's my suggestion: every 90 days, figure out a new income stream to build. Some will be trickles and some will be swift, but detach yourself from the outcome and treat every 90 days as an experiment.

Why 90 days? I've found that it's a magic amount of time, and not just because that's how calendars work. It follows the energy. Your first month is fueled entirely by enthusiasm. Your second is spent working on it, often without seeing any results, which is where a lot of people who don't commit to 90 days give up. But the third month is where the work gets rewarded in ways that you can see the future.

Committing to a 90-day experiment is simple, but not easy. That's why you have to commit first and then follow the steps. But all you really have to do is commit, pick your first 90-day experiment, and choose the easiest and most doable path for you to reach $2500 per week.

Not all of your 90-day experiments will succeed. In fact, plan on at least half of them failing. That's not to dissuade you from continuing your experiments — quite the opposite. Because in each failure you learn a great deal about your potential audience and your solution. But when you fail, fail quietly and quickly.

Here's something that I wish I could have understood sooner: the ride we're on is a roller coaster. There's no magic income level that gets you off it. If anything, each time you level up your income, you're simply switching to a bigger and more thrilling roller coaster. And just like a roller coaster, there's a low that corresponds to every high.

It's important then to know two things right now: that the roller coaster never stops, and how you handle the lows, the highs, and the in-betweens will make the difference in your life more than just about anything else you can do.

What I've found is that you can handle the highs and lows best if you measure *the right things*. Allow me to step up onto this soapbox again: most metrics people chase are vanity metrics at best and at worst, just ways to feel bad about the work they're doing. Forget page views, video downloads, subscriber count, unsubscribes. None of that matters: not now, and honestly not ever.

What should you measure?

These four things are real:

1. How many ideas did you download from your brain?

2. What are you selling?

3. How many conversations are you having about what you're selling?

4. How much cash is coming in?

Your goal is $10,000 per idea, per quarter. And if an idea earns you that money in a quarter, you know that, with consistency, you can earn that much on the idea in a month, since you've already done the building.

And when you experience success, *which you will,* an important mindset shift needs to happen in order for you to continue your successful journey. The more successful you feel, the more successful you become. This is not a cat poster slogan. This isn't leaping with the hope that the net will somehow appear. I'm not beholding the power of positive thinking or any nonsense like that. What I am saying is that people will flock to you when you start gaining momentum. So make sure to level up loudly. Take up more space. Know that the bigger you get, the more in demand you'll become, and the more people will want to be involved in what you're doing. Understand that, and don't let it cripple you.

After you're comfortably earning $10,000 a month, you've proven to yourself that this is possible, and hopefully, you'll start to see that you haven't yet reached the full capacity of your earning potential. It's sort of like what I touched on about thinking about writing a book as if you're writing your first book. So this is your first five-figure month.

It's at this point that you focus on value. How can you provide the most value for your clients? Understanding the dollar value of what you bring to the relationship is the biggest thing you can do to increase your earnings, right away. This goes beyond charging by the hour. It's not something that comes naturally to most people, and it may take a few iterations to get it right.

And yes, I know what you're thinking having read this because I've heard it before. No, really, I have — let me show you.

# MAKE A LIST OF
# YOUR 'YEAH-BUTS'

"Yosi, Michelle, and Jackie, now might be a good time to talk about the objections that are coming up. I call these the 'yeah-buts' and they're the seeds of doubt that come up even though we're taking this one ladder rung at a time. I'll grab a pen. Start calling out the 'yeah-buts' that are at the tips of your tongues." I went to get the pen and stepped over to the whiteboard.

Jackie spoke first. "No one is going to pay me for the hippie stuff I love talking about."

I wrote down, "My expertise is not something that I can monetize" and restrained myself from telling her to feel differently.

"What would I even write about?" Michelle said.

I wrote, "I don't know enough to fill a book" on the board.

143

"I'm having a hard time even thinking of myself as an expert," Yosi said.

I wrote, "Unsteady foundation" on the board.

This went on for a while, and after we'd covered what I felt was comprehensive, I stopped and looked at the board. "All of these yeah-buts are valid. I could respond to each of them, but I'm not sure that would be beneficial, and honestly, I don't think my responses would come across as anything other than defensive posturing anyway."

"So instead of responding to each objection now, I'll simply say this: your job, today, is to decide. Decide that this is the path you want to take and that it's possible for you too. I know that might not be satisfying to hear, but deciding is so important that it bears repeating."

Michelle piped up: "Today felt heavier than yesterday. Maybe because yesterday we downloaded our ideas. That left me feeling lighter. Thinking about the money feels bigger — denser and way more real. And while that's great, it's also incredibly intimidating. What if I'm wrong? What if the things I thought I wanted to talk about yesterday, the ideas swimming around in my head, what if that's not the direction I want to take my life? What if, I don't know, I want to help people file their taxes?"

I smiled. "It's normal to feel *massive resistance* at this stage. Because what we've been working on this weekend are big, life-altering decisions. We'll talk about this later but just remember: what we came up with this weekend are the first sparks.

Your first ideas. They don't have to be THE thing you settle on. Out of curiosity, do you love doing taxes?"

She grinned. "I most certainly do not! In fact, I hate them. I think what I'm feeling is that my expertise is in such a pedestrian thing, that maybe I should get better at other things instead."

"Ah!" I said. "I felt the same way. Marketing, my expertise, isn't even *a thing* — it's a vehicle in which to sell other things. So I had to do a lot of work to come around to the idea that my expertise is in fact in something that matters."

She laughed. "Are you serious, or just trying to make me feel better? Marketing is most certainly a thing!"

I nodded, very serious now. "When I went through these weekend exercises the first time, I struggled. Really struggled. On day one, my notebook was filled with the most defeatist language you can imagine. 'I don't know anything, I've never known anything, nothing I do know is anything I can turn into a business, maybe people don't even *need* marketing...' — that kind of thing. You might laugh. But because the things we're good at come so easily to us, we devalue them. Take the idea you keep coming back to. Who wouldn't want a house they could feel less anxiety about, especially when it comes to connecting with people they care about?"

She nodded. "Good point. A clean house makes me feel good. But it doesn't change the world."

145

"Oh, but it does. In fact, since we're on the topic of changing the world, know this: you're off the hook for changing 'the world.' One person acting alone cannot change the world at large. But you can make life better for your corner of the world, and that's something."

"Plus, it's important to understand that you don't have to decide this weekend how you're going to spend the rest of your life. You just have to decide to launch an experiment and commit to that experiment for three months."

Yosi piped up. "I get it. We're off the hook for changing the world and off the hook for making a decision this weekend that will impact the rest of our lives. It is helpful to hear that. Because it vastly reduces what it is I'm supposed to focus on and makes it something that I can do. Right now, I have one job, and that's to commit to the process."

"That's right," I said. "You don't have to earn a single dollar, not this weekend anyway. You just have to end the day with insights into positioning yourself for earning."

As dinner time was right around the corner, we piled into a Lyft so we didn't have to worry about parking and wandered around downtown Scottsdale for a bit. I'd forgotten how fun it was to be a tourist, and wandering through art galleries and turquoise and silver shops with people who'd never been here before was a lot of fun. Despite the day two resistance, everyone seemed relaxed.

After we ordered dinner, the chitchat died down. "We talked about resistance earlier this afternoon. Is anyone else still feeling it?"

"I am," Yosi offered. "I still think to myself, if only I knew things that could *really* change the world, instead of the pedestrian things that I actually know. Yesterday I felt like my ideas could light the world up, and today, right now, I feel very differently. Like a balloon with a tiny pinprick in it."

I nodded. "Then I think you'll like the direction this evening's conversation will take. I want to assure you that those feelings — your ideas are small, and only big ideas will bring you money — are completely normal. You're in good company here."

Everyone laughed. "It's true," I said. "And it happens at every weekend workshop I facilitate. Day one is build-up, day two is about showing the possibilities, and then, invariably, during the afternoon, everything comes shattering down. Is that what you feel?"

Everyone nodded.

Our drinks arrived, along with the appetizers we ordered.

"Let's raise a glass," I said. "To the breakdown that is necessary before the inevitable rebuild!"

"Cheers to that!"

"Cheers!"

Glasses clinked.

# RECOGNIZING THE RESISTANCE

The feelings of inadequacy that Yosi, Michelle, and Jackie feel are simply those of resistance showing up in different ways. Resistance will always be there, but there are two ways you can work through it. What I like to do when I feel resistance, especially in a Mindshop environment like this — one where things are 100% set up for you to succeed — is two-fold.

First, acknowledge the resistance. Say hello to it. 'Hello, resistance. Welcome. You can have a seat right here next to me.' When I do that, it dissipates more easily, and I know why. I'm no longer spending any mental energy trying *not* to feel. Instead, I'm letting it sit there.

Second, I realize that the resistance is there because I'm doing something scary. 'I know you're here to keep me safe,'

I'll say. 'But I am safe, so I'm going to push anyway. This is truly the only way I'll grow.'

It helps to verbalize these statements after you've written them down, which is why I wouldn't recommend it if you're going to work at a restaurant or a coffee shop. But I'm completely serious when I say that if you talk to it, comfort it, and make it your friend, it will lose its power over you. And yes, I did say comfort it — the resistance you are feeling is the thing that's actually scared, not you. You're ready to take the leap. You just need to reassure resistance that you'll be okay.

This book is intended to show you the possibility of making such a leap. But it's not like you're Evel Knievel jumping across the Grand Canyon — this is not a life sentence. You don't even have to declare your major or map out the rest of your life. Mapping can feel really great, but can also feel like a prison sentence, even if you're the mapmaker, which you are. Even if you're doing something you love.

But resistance is another way we keep ourselves from doing the next important step. Resistance tells you that you might *not* want to become known for the things you wrote down yesterday. Resistance leaps 30 years ahead and shows you the Ghost of Expertise Future. And that's not okay — because the world needs your expertise. Trust me on this.

Understand where the resistance is coming from, and know that all you need to do is to break your future into 90-day intervals. Stop worrying about the long term and focus instead on the next step.

As the meal progressed, Yosi turned to me. "Okay, you don't want us to worry about the long term. What do you propose we worry about instead?"

I grinned. "What you'll focus on instead of the long term is launching quarterly experiments. You don't have to decide what you'll do forever, but you do need to commit to a project you'll pour yourself into for the next 90 days. All it takes is figuring out what to launch each quarter."

"How do we determine what we're going to launch each quarter, and what does that even look like?" Yosi asked.

"The execution will look different every time. But you'll determine which problem you'll focus on, who you'll help, and how you'll do that."

"So you launch experiments. And every experiment asks the same question: can I earn $10,000 doing this?"

"Then you do all you can in a 90-day period to see whether that combination is viable. By the end of the quarter, you'll have an answer. And you can tweak any of your variables for the next quarter."

"I feel like you're letting us off the hook!" Michelle said.

"Is it really that easy? Just pick something, then focus on it for three months?" Jackie asked. "I can do anything for three months!"

Jackie isn't wrong but she's not entirely right either. Yes, 90-day experiments are what you need to create. But that means selecting ONE PROJECT to focus on for 90 days. Really test your idea and see if it'll eventually become a $10,000 one. If you ultimately don't believe this life can work for you, then you won't work toward making it true.

MINDSTORM

18

# THREE LEVELS OF BELIEF

There are three levels to this belief. The first is that it's possible to make that kind of money on knowledge and information. I can give you examples of people who are doing it in every niche. If you don't believe me, look up "top influencers" and add an industry.

The second level is that it's possible for you to make this kind of money on your knowledge and ideas. That's where a lot of people get stuck. That's why we spent Parts One and Two Mindstorming and narrowing your expertise down to some concrete ideas.

But the third is that you can do this now. You don't have to wait for some arbitrary date. You don't need to go get a certification. It's the willingness to jump in and run your first experiment without the certainty of a soft landing. Overcoming doubt is a challenge, and it's not something you can tick off a to-do list. It's something you have to work on, constantly.

Building a life around your own ideas is a decision and a commitment. Maybe you thought you'd instead get some ideas reading this book and could test out a hobby and find a way to make a few dollars in your spare time. But that's the wrong mindset. In order to make this work, you have to be the gardener of your own mind. You have to cut the other branches so this one can bear the best fruit. You have to decide who you're going to help, and how you're going to help them. And you have to decide to make it work by committing to the entire journey.

And let me be clear about one final thing. This journey isn't all about the money. It's about doing good work with people you really want to help. So when those feelings of inadequacy come up, and oh, they will, just remember that the more successful you become, the more people you can help.

My best advice is to surround yourself with other people going through the same thing you're going through. Connect with them, follow them, and most of all support them. A rising tide lifts all boats, so see what sort of help you can provide while you build. The important thing to know is that there are tough spots, some points in the journey are harder than others, and none of them are the ones you expect.

Oh, and there's one more piece of advice I give to anyone taking a Mindshop with me.

"One final thing you need to know is what we're doing this weekend, what we're working toward, what we're building... it's going to be fun, but it's not a hobby."

"What do you mean?" Jackie asked.

"I'll use Yosi as an example, and discuss her expertise, specifically regarding Instagram." I turned to Yosi. "Tell me about what it felt like when you first discovered Instagram."

Yosi brightened. "I remember being *so excited* to have an iPhone because back in the day, Instagram was only available on iOS. So I got to figure out how it worked. I spent hours — days, probably — fiddling with the different filters, all the hidden features, everything. It was the digital version of taking the toaster apart and putting it back together. I loved it."

I nodded. "That's what I expected you'd say. Often our hobbies become viable opportunities for revenue. But the moment you decide that you're going to turn your expertise into something that will earn you money, the paradigm necessarily shifts. And this isn't necessarily a good or bad thing, but as soon as you start thinking about building a business around something you've kept as a hobby, you have to start thinking about it differently. That's not to say don't monetize your hobbies. I'm saying that the moment you decide to monetize them, they're no longer hobbies. And monetizing something you love can be really fun. You'll look up one day and realize you're getting paid for this." I gestured around.

"But it's no longer a hobby. It's now a way more important part of your life than just a hobby. And you'll find that you won't want to 'play' with it anymore, outside of your work time. So, find other pastimes for your enjoyment."

"My final piece of advice before I let you off the hook for the evening," I said as we waited for our Lyft to bring us back, "is to remember that this new way of life isn't as clear of a separation between work and home as you're accustomed to. It's a combination of both, and by monetizing your knowledge, you're showing the people around you just how possible it is to have the life you want. So think about what that looks like, and I'll see you in the morning."

# PART 4:

# BUILDING YOUR MARKETING ENGINE

## WHAT IS A MARKETING ENGINE?

In these final two parts, we're going to tie everything together. Remember our three-legged stool? On each leg there were words. The first was *expertise*. The second was *positioning*. And on the third was *marketing engine*.

Part One was all about finding and refining our expertise. Parts Two and Three were about thinking about how to position ourselves to monetize quickly. Those three parts were all about where we're going. Having figured that out, we're going to spend the rest of the book talking about how we're going to build a marketing engine to take us there.

These are my favorite parts because here's where the rubber meets the road and you really get to see your ideas come to fruition. I'm not just a dreamer, and I know you aren't either. I'm 100% in favor of dreaming big, but I'm also all about executing those dreams. Unfortunately, so many people are taught how to dream big, but no one then explains how to make those dreams become a reality.

And so I want to take the next two parts to help you build a marketing engine to get you there. What do I mean by a marketing engine? It's the machine that helps you build your brand, establish you as the authority that you are, and helps you scale your income online. There are five components to a marketing engine:

1. Your website

2. Your sales page

3. Your opt-in

4. Your emails

5. And finally your content

When properly assembled it's a remarkable engine that can truly power your fantastic ideas and get them noticed. But since they are your ideas, it's worth pausing a second to explain why these elements of your marketing engine are where you should put your energy. In a word, they are *yours*. Here's how I put it to the three women at the Mindshop:

"Allow me to step up on my metaphorical soapbox again. Here's what I want to say: The internet is a strange and wonderful place, but there are so few places where you own anything. You're a renter on almost all the real estate."

"Real estate? What do you mean?" Jackie asked.

"I mean, be careful where you build. Let's say someone came to you and said, 'Hey, would you like to build your house on this beautiful piece of land? It's adjacent to the ocean, has highway access, and anything you'd build would be automatically retrofitted for earthquakes. And I can get you deals with builders. In fact, you can start building, right now, *for free*. There's just one catch: I still own the land."

"Would you build?"

They all shook their heads. "No, of course not," Michelle said. "I'm not going to spend time building something, even if there are deals to be had, if I don't own the land."

"No way, me neither," Yosi chimed in, "and in fact, if someone came to me with an offer like that, I would be immediately suspicious."

Jackie was quiet. "What do you think?" I asked her.

"I think," she replied, "you're talking about social media. Instagram. TikTok. Facebook ads. Twitter. Even LinkedIn.

Places where we can get banned, demoted, or removed without so much as a heads up."

I nodded. "You're absolutely right, Jackie. And because of that, you absolutely must be an owner, not a renter, on the vast majority of your online content. You own your website and you own your email list. Those are two places you should devote most of your time and energy."

Yosi looked discouraged. I turned to her. "I'm not saying don't focus on Instagram, especially since you are so invested in your Instagram work. I'm saying to have a repository for your content that does not depend on another company like Instagram. When you add something to Instagram, make sure you're adding it to your website too."

She nodded. "That makes good sense. It's counterintuitive, especially since so many influencers I know are *only* on Instagram."

"I know people like that, too. And to tie it back to my analogy, it might be the case that the person who owns the land is some sort of benevolent landlord who never asks for rent and never kicks you off the property. But there's no guarantee of that, and what's worse, as you build your house (or Instagram influence), you don't have any control over what you (after a time) come to consider your own."

I mimed stepping off the soapbox. "Now that that's done, let's get started."

## REGISTER YOURNAME.COM

If you're anything like me, you go from idea to URL in about five seconds. By that, I mean that I know plenty of people who have dozens (if not hundreds) of domains registered. Every time they have an idea, they go register that domain. And a year later, when it comes up for renewal, they have no idea what they were thinking when inspiration hit. Often, the domain simply stays registered, and they are out of pocket another sum for a domain name they will never ever use.

Because you're intentionally running 90-day experiments, it doesn't make any sense to be investing in domain names during that window. But you do need a domain. So let yourself off the proverbial hook and do this instead: register "your name dot com."

Doing that makes so much more sense for a variety of reasons. The first is the most obvious: because no matter what you end up doing, it'll be *you* doing it. So if Jackie starts talking about Reiki, and then switches to talking about plant-based eating, that's fine. Because people will be seeking her out for her opinions on things.

But if she registers JackieLovesReiki.com but then pivots in a quarter to talk about how to eat more plants, she'll feel like she can't use her first URL. So she goes and gets JackieLovesPlants.com too. Now she has two sites. Two content calendars. Two places to focus. And two websites is one website too many. I've seen this happen dozens of times, and

I want to spare you the heartache of wasting all that time. Get your name. Or some variation of your name. You are not simply the face of your brand. You *are* your brand.

Let me share with you how I explained it to the women at my Mindshop because it's one of the only times I use a prop to make my point. I picked up a book I brought with me to make this very point: *Keep Going* by Austin Kleon.

"Are you familiar with this writer?" I asked.

"I loved his *Steal Like an Artist* book," Yosi said. I nodded. "Me too," I said. "It helped me get over the idea of having to have original thoughts and gave me the perspective that even if my take wasn't 100% my own, I had something important to add to the conversation."

"He's a prolific writer. He writes five posts per week on his blog, about all kinds of different things: what he's reading, what he's writing about, what's going on in his town, all of it. But what really surprised me was that he mentioned once on Twitter that he didn't have Google Analytics installed on his website. I couldn't get over it. I used to write on my blog every day, which for me translated checking analytics obsessively after posting what I wrote. As if Google could tell me whether or not my stuff was worth reading. And here's this writer with three published books and a journal who *never even knows* what his traffic looks like."

"I'm not sure I could do that," Jackie said. "I mean, I want to know if what I'm putting out there is getting seen at all." I nodded. "I'm with you. I have it installed, but these days

I rarely look at it. Because he has a point. His point, which I've heard from offline writers, is that daily writing is the point. Creating is the point. Everything else is unnecessary to track. Plus, we have the other metric: whether or not we're picking up clients. Be careful not to get so focused on whether your content resonates that you forget to do the one thing that will help you move the needle: make money."

"And so with Austin Kleon as our guide, let's move forward. What you're creating when you build a website is the modern equivalent of a three-fold brochure. Remember those?"

Everyone nodded. "I still get them occasionally in the mail even," Michelle said.

"Yup — the classic junk mail. We're building internet junk mail."

There were chuckles all around.

"But in all seriousness, before I start talking about the components of your website, I want to say something valuable about junk mail. It's this: it's easy to build and easy to reconfigure. You'll want to build your website as fast as possible. A decent website should not cost the same as a reliable used car, nor should it take longer to build than it takes to grow a baby. The world moves so fast that every two years you're going to need to 'trade in' and redesign your site, which you will not want to do if you spent $30,000 and ten months designing it in the first place. Keep that in mind over the course of our discussion about the different parts of your website: whatever you build will not be what's standing at the end because there is no end state for your website — just like junk mail never stops coming either!"

They all laughed, but they understood my point. And that brings me to one final point I want to get out of the way when talking about your website. Since I've convinced you to hang your shingle on your name dot com, you'll need to take some pictures of your face. A brand photoshoot, if you will.

Now before you run for the hills, let me make my case. People do business with people, so you will need to show your face. Especially since you've decided on your name dot com. Because at the end of the day, they are doing business with you, so you better get used to you being the face of your brand.

Even in my business, where I'm one of two partners with a team of independent contractors, I have to show my face online. Every single piece of content we put out that has either my face or my cofounder's face gets *ten times the engagement* compared to any other image.

I'm not saying that you need to be cute or cutesy unless you want to. But I am saying you need to put yourself out there, and that means a series of branded photos. You need a 'good enough' set of pics, so make plans in the next 24 hours to get that done by reaching out to a friend to take photos of each other. All you need is one shot in natural lighting that makes you look professional, approachable, and fun.

Now let's talk about the five basic pages on a website.

# WRITE COPY FOR
# YOUR HOME PAGE

Aside from a picture of yourself, on your homepage you'll want to add:

- **A headline:** What's the overarching benefit people can expect from you while they're browsing your site?

- **A tagline:** What, in a few words, can people expect from your website?

- **A call to action:** Give them something to download, some way to connect with you.

- **Content blocks:** Ways they can go deeper, more about you and what you're about.

- **Testimonials:** As early as possible, get people who aren't you to tell the world how great you are.

I know that sounds like a lot, and I'm sure you have questions about each part, but I want to do an activity first. In the spirit of stealing like an artist, what I'd like you to do is find a website of someone way outside your niche and use it as inspiration. To be clear, I'm not asking you to plagiarize their ideas nor steal their format. This is not going to wind up being your page. I just want you to start flexing your copywriting skills. If you're uncomfortable then head to my page: amplifiedNOW.com. I hereby give you permission to use it as a jumping-off point.

Getting inspiration is important for a very obvious reason. When you start to create your own home page, you might be surprised by the writer's block you feel. It's one thing to generate content but quite another to do so when trying to format it all at the same time. Learning to build a website is enough of a lift — you don't want to have to flex your creative writing muscles at the same time. Best then to sort out first what it is you want to say so you can concentrate on the layout when building the page.

So pull up that web page and start rewriting it now. You'll be surprised at how much you have to say, and how unique it will be.

# WRITE COPY FOR
# YOUR ABOUT PAGE

Your About page is the next most important page on your website. If you've written the copy correctly on your home page, you'll inspire people to do one of three things:

- Decide they don't want to work with you
- Decide they *do* want to work with you
- Need a little more information and context about whether or not to work with you

That might sound like your homepage failed — certainly my Mindshop participants thought it sounded like a potential failure — so I want you to hear what I told them:

"Shouldn't we try to make our copy on our main page appeal to everyone so people don't leave our site so fast?" Yosi asked.

"That's a good instinct, but no. The smaller and narrower your niche, the easier it will be to attract the people you want to attract, and by doing your best work attracting the right people, the wrong people will simply leave. That's the goal."

"But don't we want to attract people to our site to build up our numbers?" Jackie asked.

"You would if you were tracking your numbers. But building up your numbers is not what you want to do here. Do you want to field a bunch of inquiries from people who are kinda/sorta/maybe interested in what you're doing, or would you rather just know that when someone writes they are truly interested in what you have to offer? Your homepage, therefore, is a filtering mechanism for those who are in or who are out. But not everyone will make a decision based just on it. That's why you have an About page."

"Writing about myself really intimidates me," Michelle said.

"Oh, it should. It's like having to write a resume, only online. And writing a resume is a big challenge."

Everyone nodded so vigorously I thought their heads might fall off.

"Isn't part of the reason to explore entrepreneurship to opt-out of resume updating once and for all?"

"Yes, definitely," I said. "But you do need one. So here's a great trick to help you: your About page *isn't* about you."

"It's not?" Jackie asked. "Then what exactly is it about?"

"Yeah!" Michelle said. "Where are you supposed to start? This weekend? Birth? Somewhere in between? What's important to share?"

"You're getting to the crux of why this kind of writing is *really hard* for a lot of people," I said. "But keep in mind that you're now focused on a certain group of people who go to About pages. Those that know you're not the person for them have left. Those who know you are the right person have already decided. The only people who are left are those that are looking for reasons to do business with you."

I handed out another piece of paper. This one was mostly blank. Across the top was the headline "About How I Can Help You."

"So now it's not about you, not really. It's about you in the context of how you can help the person visiting your site for the first time. Take your backstory, Jackie. Your story starts just before you found out what plant-based eating could do for you. What was your life like before your moment of transformation?"

"Why does that part of the story matter?" Jackie wondered aloud.

"Because," I replied, "without it, there's no empathy. I know you wouldn't do this because it's not in your nature, but you're stunning and fit and radiate this inner beauty, so your page could, if left unchecked, come across as sanctimonious."

The look on her face was one of understanding. "Thank you for the compliment, and I understand what you mean. If I get nice headshots and write about the energy of the universe and plant-based eating, some people won't believe I'm a normal person who is glad that Oreos are vegan because sometimes I can eat six of them at once."

"Yes!" I said. "It's going to be important for you to prove to your readers that you're just like them."

I looked at the others. "This advice holds true for everyone. You're building a practice around your expertise, and by definition, you're an expert in topics other people aren't, so in order to gain someone's trust, you need to give what I'll call 'six Oreo' examples. If you were born into royalty, and you want to teach people how to be a prince, they're not going to think they can learn anything from you, because your first step would be: 'step one: be born into a royal family' and that excludes just about the whole world."

Michelle chuckled. "Unless, of course, your name is Aladdin."

"Of course," Yosi said.

"Right, but if you set yourself up so that you're teaching people how to do the thing that you know they can do, then your About page is simply a collection of lines to talk about how you are like the people you are here to help. And if you can't explain to them how you can help them, well, then I think it's fair to think that you can't. But if you think back to our Mindstorming about ideas, it's pretty clear that everyone was overflowing with ideas about how they could help. That's all your About page is really about."

"And remember: like with every page on your website, write it now and then let it go and move on because, in three or six months, you're going to revisit it anyway and adjust it based on what your business has looked like in the last quarter or two."

With that advice in mind, let's get you to write some bullet points right now for your About page. Be sure to cover your insight or transformation. Don't neglect to mention your expertise. And share those six Oreo moments.

Don't be afraid to show your personality. Don't be shy about shining a light on what you're good at. Just give your reader a list of things that will let people know that you're someone they want to do business with.

At this juncture, it makes sense to actually start building your site. I don't have much advice, since I've only ever built sites on WordPress, but I know there are plenty of other great website builders out there.

The point is to get your website done to a point where you're comfortable showing it to other people and then move on. A website is a destination of sorts. But it's step zero. Which is why I don't want you to spend too much time on it. You need one, of course. But it's far more important to get people to come to your site than it is to have a perfect website from day one.

MINDSTORM

21

# WRITE YOUR FIRST SALES PAGE

You are welcome to spend as much time as you want making your site perfect. But for now, let's agree that your site so far is where it needs to be and move right on to reverse designing the most important page of your website — your marketing engine — also known as your **Sales Page**.

Or as I explained it to the women in the Mindshop, in order to move forward we're going to have to move backward.

I handed out a piece of paper with this diagram on it:

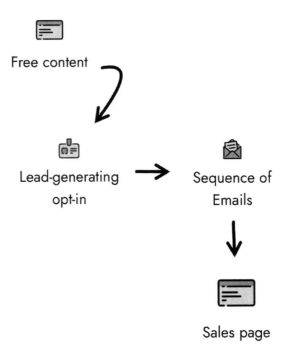

"These are the blocks of a marketing engine, and when I say we're going to work backward, all I mean is we're going to design with the end in mind, which means we should start at the end with the sales page."

"Hang on, I already have a question," Yosi said. "Isn't this a sales funnel? And if so, where are the Facebook ads?"

"I suppose you could call this a sales funnel, but I don't like that imagery," I replied. "Think about it: what does a funnel do?"

"Gets things into a bottle," Michelle said. "At least in my house."

"Right," Jackie said. "Forcing liquid into a restricted space."

"Exactly," I said. "The thing that gets my hackles up is the idea of forcing your website visitor to do something. Left alone, the liquid would expand into a larger space, but a funnel makes it do something that it wouldn't naturally do. That feels wrong to me, and I daresay feels wrong to the user as well, and it is part of the reason marketing gets a bad rap."

"Now, what comes to mind when you imagine a marketing engine instead of a sales funnel?"

"Well, it sounds like we need to build it," Michelle said.

"And power it?" Yosi chimed in.

"Right. And to answer your question, the fuel we feed it is traffic. But you don't buy gas before you have somewhere to put it, which is why we're not going to talk about that today. And to be perfectly honest, in the ever-changing world of paid traffic, whatever is working today won't necessarily be the thing that works tomorrow. A lot of people who have created something want to *start* with paid advertising. But it's important to remember that ads are fuel, and you can't just pour fuel on your website. So let's set aside the fuel question and focus on the build. Does that make sense?"

"It does," Michelle said. "So the first thing we need to write is the sales page."

"Indeed," I said. "This is the strategic approach: let's figure out where your people are ultimately going, then work backward from there."

"You probably know where I'm going next," I said, "but I'm going to state it anyway: writing your own sales page brings up all kinds of bad feelings for a lot of people. Especially right now, when you haven't even put the finishing touches on the thing you want to sell. So I want to teach you an easy and less painful way to put it together."

I handed out my sales page template that is covered with different prompts. "This is what I use every single time I'm writing a new sales page," I said.

Michelle looked dubious. "It's just a bunch of bullet points," she said. "Does it really help you? Do you write sales pages in this kind of template style?"

"I do," I said. "Every single time. And it's safe to say I've written hundreds of sales pages. I'm not saying any of this is flawless or foolproof. But it does have a solid track record. So let's start writing your sales page."

"What, you mean now?" Jackie asked. "Before we've even finished creating our thing?"

"Absolutely. In fact, *always* start the sales page before you finish creating."

"Why?" Yosi asked.

"Because it's like a GPS device guiding you to the finish line, with the sales page telling you your destination. Once you know where you're going, getting there becomes a simple matter of following the steps. Writing the sales page will show you exactly what you need to create. You can use it as an outline when you're creating your thing, and you'll be a big step ahead once you finish."

"That seems... counterintuitive," Michelle said.

"You're right. But it's not the first counterintuitive thing you've heard this weekend, so let me show you how this plays out. Once you get the hang of it, writing your sales pages becomes part of your product development process. You'll see what you need to create by following the outline."

You have the outline in front of you in the workbook, so let me simply walk you through the steps. The first bullet is to articulate a **pain point**. It should be short and concise. Five to ten words (max) that will draw your reader in. Ask a question or make a statement that captures their most intense desire or fear. This is a headline. The first thing people see on your sales page. The thing that makes them decide whether to keep reading or leave. Make your bold promise, ask a provocative question, get right to the heart of the person reading this.

Then you'll write about their fears. Remember that sales copy is all about transformation. What does the future look like for your reader if they don't change? Describe the status quo: the now or **before picture**. Write a paragraph that goes down that rabbit hole. Use words like tired, weary, exhausted, drained, flagging, ragged.

Then talk about their desires. What does the world look like for them after they transform? Not just after they buy what you're selling, but after they decide to take action on this particular pain point? What sorts of rainbows appear? Where's the ray of light? In this section, it's really important to get them to visualize themselves in the excellent **after picture**. Use words and phrases like imagine, what if, think, suppose, visualize. Use this section to get them ready for your offer because it's coming next.

Immediately after this, **introduce your offer**. In a headline. Use the phrase 'welcome to' or 'introducing' followed by the name of your offer. Use the working name for now. You can always replace it later. Then describe in a few words exactly what that offer provides. Think of this as the subheading or tagline — a quick description of what it can do for your reader.

After this, you get to be quiet for a second and let someone else's words tell your reader just how great you are. Remember that you don't have to have testimonials from people who have been through the exact thing you're writing the sales page about. But you do have to have a **first testimonial** from people who know how great *you* are, and you can use those for now.

Next up is the **value claim**. Reiterate exactly what your offer will give them. Reword your subtitle and use that here. Then start talking about your product in terms of what your buyer will get. Remember that no one is moved to buy the means by which the transformation happens, be it videos or worksheets. They buy the transformation. So don't tell them about the Facebook group or one-on-one call without context. Translate them into value statements. The group becomes a community of like-minded people. The one-on-one calls become personalized guidance from an expert — that kind of thing. Talk through what will happen as a result of taking you up on your offer.

You'll want to break up your sales page at this point with a **second testimonial**. I like to think of it as a conversation. When one person drones on and on and on for too long, people get restless. On a sales page, it means we need to add different voices or we'll lose our readers. So here's another opportunity for a testimonial.

At this point you've set up your offer and explained it a bit, some people will be convinced to buy, or at least curious about the price point. Also, people like clicking things. So, add a **buy button** here and let them click if they want to.

It's only at this point once you've added a buy button on the sales page that you **introduce yourself**. Add another photo of yourself, so they can put a face on the offer. This introduction is even easier to write than your About page. The format is easy: your name and your topline LinkedIn bio.

Then a paragraph or two on your personal story. Your before picture, your a-ha moment, your transformation, and the steps you took. End with your realization that if this could work for you, you could help other people achieve the same transformation.

Then comes the section where you **qualify people**. If I could have a favorite section when writing a sales page, this would be it. This is the point at which you start talking about who would get the most benefit from your offer, and sometimes who wouldn't. Lead with a headline using this formula or something like it: 'You are too [something positive] to [not have the result I'm selling on this page].' They're too smart, vibrant, full of potential, to keep from transforming. Then you have bullet points talking about your ideal customer. Who is right for your offer? What do they have in common? What are they tired of? What do they fear? What demographic details do they share? Then if it makes sense, create a section about who is wrong for your offer. Who shouldn't buy? For these people, it's the same lack of readiness pattern: if you're willing to stay in your crappy situation, if you're not willing to put in the time and effort, etc. But oftentimes that comes across as too negative and I cut it.

Then come the **details**. It too is a fun page to write, especially for creators who don't have a lot of experience writing conversion-oriented copy. Here you'll come up with a list of bullet points telling people exactly what they're getting. And this section is why I write a sales page early in the product creation process — to see if what I have in my head looks like a robust enough offer. This is also the place for the mechanics: this is the place where you talk about the number and format of your classes. How many modules? How many coaching sessions? Talk about the worksheets. The assignments. The homework. Where will your community be meeting? Be crystal clear so you can avoid miscommunication down the line. Outline exactly what you're going to deliver. Is it a membership? How long does it last? What are the deliverables?

I know the page feels like it's getting pretty long, but these moves are key to converting customers. The next section is about returning to the **'before' picture** and **pain point** again, so refer back to those sections. Start with a headline that says something along the lines of 'you can keep doing what you're doing' then draw out what happens if they decide not to transform. Make it really uncomfortable — to be truly valuable, your offer needs to solve a particularly painful pain point — one that people will pay money to solve. So what happens if they don't solve it? What falls apart in their life? What breaks down? This section ends with some sort of phrase like 'if you don't take this pain point seriously, something bad will happen. And nobody deserves a life full of that pain point.'

Then comes your third and final testimonial followed by the second buy button. At this point they've been reading — or let's be honest, skimming — for a bit. Give them another testimonial, and then another chance to click and buy right after the third testimonial.

That's the end of what I consider the required elements of a sales page. There are just a couple more optional sections I want to share with you because they might help you in creating your offer, but they truly are optional.

The first is **outlines or screenshots of what's inside**. Don't skip this if you haven't outlined your offer yet. On a lot of sales pages, people will show a full module-by-module outline of their digital product. The other thing you'll see are screenshots of worksheets on different-sized devices. You won't be able to create those until you've created the worksheets, but writing the outline (if you haven't done it yet) is really helpful. You can see your outline in context with everything else you've written so far and see if it aligns with your messaging.

A section devoted to **FAQs** is another optional section. You won't have any questions yet, but it's a useful way to think about objections. What are some of the reasons people might not buy your offer? What are some of the questions you can anticipate? Think beyond obvious softball questions like, 'how on earth is this not twice the price?' and you'll be rewarded. If some of the questions you come up with reveal a missing piece of your offer, at least you know now so you can course correct.

The final section you could include is a pricing table at the bottom of the sales page. When people click the buy buttons earlier on the page, I navigate them here because when you give people a pricing table, you're changing the conversation from whether they should buy from you to which option provides them with the best fit. It's an important distinction. Offer three options: the one you want to provide, the one that's easiest to provide, and the one that you don't want too many people to choose. The easiest one is your least expensive option. The one you want is the middle, and the one you really don't want gets priced at the highest price, which will serve as an anchor and will pay you enough so you don't get upset when someone does buy that option.

# PART 5:

# FUELING YOUR MARKETING ENGINE

# CREATE YOUR FIRST
# LEAD-GENERATING OPT-IN

Remember the diagram from a few pages ago? We built the endpoint. Now, all we need to do is create a lead-generating opt-in — something free and enticing that will grab the attention of potential buyers.

Once we have that, we can create the emails that go along with it. Then, and only then, we can start sending traffic to it.

We build an opt-in because sending a cold audience — that is, an audience who's never heard of you — to a sales page and hope that some people buy won't work. I mean, it's *technically* possible, but it's not a good use of your money. Instead, you need to warm them up. And that's what a lead-generating opt-in does. It's the thing that you can send paid traffic to that introduces the people who have the problem that your offer solves and ask only that they give up their email address in order to get it. Once someone joins your email list, they are no longer cold traffic. They're warm now. They're getting to know you.

The women at the Mindshop certainly jelled with that idea. Michelle nodded, understanding why she needed to build a lead-generating opt-in. "It's a bit like dating, I suppose. And you can't come on too strong when you first meet someone or you'll scare them away, right?"

"That's exactly it," I said. "Jackie, would you continue the metaphor?"

"So… the opt-in would be some sort of a line on your dating profile that said 'if you swipe right, I'll give you a piece of candy'? Is that where you were going with this?"

We all laughed. "I mean, we already said we were populating the internet with more junk mail," Yosi said. "Why not become the stranger in the car our parents warned us about?"

"We can all agree that Michelle's metaphor is a good one to get us started, but isn't one we can use to talk about warming up our traffic. But maybe we don't need a metaphor for this. What we need to create is that first entry point. A freebie. Some in the industry call them lead magnets because of their intent to attract the right kind of people."

Yosi gave me a quizzical look. "What do you mean when you say the 'right kind' of people?" she asked.

"Let's take a look at giveaways for an example of what I mean," I said. "Giveaways are a great way to build some buzz and attention. But you have to be careful about what you're giving away. Your instinct might be to give away a $100 Amazon gift card, or if you really want to build buzz, an iPad. But you don't want to do that."

"Why not?" Michelle asked. "Everyone could use a $100 gift card."

"That's precisely why!" I said. "You don't want the whole world to sign up for your email list. You only want people who have the problem your offer solves to sign up for your list. Because otherwise you're building a list for the sake of building a list, and the only thing that will do is increase the amount of money you're paying to your email service provider. So instead, think about the person who actually wants what you're ultimately selling."

And in the business the three women and you are going to build, there is no better way to attract the "right" sort of people than by offering a webinar.

## YOUR FIRST OPT-IN IS AN ON-DEMAND WEBINAR

In its essence, a webinar is essentially a person narrating a slide deck. That makes it sound dry as toast, but it's quite a bit more than that. It's a presentation that showcases your knowledge and abilities — in fact, it showcases *you*. It shows your buyers what it's like to work with you. It gives viewers a feel for what you're like, whether your teaching style resonates with them, and whether they want to work with you. An on-demand webinar is excellent for all industries, but especially those where you're highlighting your expertise then asking people to commit to working with you.

I've built my business around webinars, and I create them for clients, and every single one I've built has resulted in more leads, more brand awareness, more email subscribers, and most importantly, more sales. The best part is, you can create one that runs in the background, collecting leads while you're doing other things.

Let's talk about the different parts of a webinar, and how they all work together. Of course, before you even design your webinar you need the **topic**. There are two that work really well.

One is mistakes. What are the different types of mistakes your target audience makes when they're not transforming? While it might sound kind of negative, it doesn't have to be. In Jackie's case, maybe it's the six mistakes most people make when they're transitioning to a plant-based life. That's not so much as negative as trying to be helpful, but it does pique a person's interest. They come across that headline and think, 'Hmm, I don't think I'm making any mistakes, but I can't be sure,' and they sign up.

The other topic that works really well is a step-by-step process on how to accomplish the thing your offer does. For Michelle, that would be the five steps to making cleaning with kids fun and productive. She can take the outline of her course and teach the high-level parts.

Ask a few **questions at the beginning** to help center them, and know whether they're in the right place. Leading questions, because this is marketing, not law. *Are you this type of person with that type of problem? Do you wish you didn't have to worry about something?*

The **outline/teaching portion** is where I see a lot of entrepreneurs flounder. Typically it's a lack of confidence that compels them to overcompensate by getting way too into the weeds about their system, or their background, or their approach. So go put a tight framework around the common mistakes so that everything you say is the same "bite-size" — maybe limit the length of each step in the step-by-step approach to a two-minute description.

Then you'll offer them the **decision point**. It'll look something like this:

*Now, the way I see it, you have two options. The first is the DIY approach. On your own, // take these steps that I laid out for you, and do them, one by one // make sure you're not making these most common mistakes. // This is the slower approach. If you're the kind of person who likes to DIY things — maybe you're the person who follows YouTube videos when your sink springs a leak — then simply follow the steps I've outlined today and do it. But if you're the kind of person who calls a professional when something breaks at home, and you want a little more accountability...*

After you're happy with your slides, then record yourself talking through them. Embed that recording on your site, gate it with a form, and you have your first opt-in!

Only, you're not done. Now, you have some emails to write. They're not so hard, as you'll see in this next section.

You're allowed to create multiple opt-ins, but only after you've finished the first one. You can create a PDF checklist, or even a quiz. But do this one first, then see how it works. After that, create your next one(s).

# WRITE A SEQUENCE OF EMAILS, CONNECTING YOUR OPT-IN TO YOUR SALES PAGE

"I'm excited to talk about emails!" Michelle said.

"I'm happy to hear that," I said, "though a little surprised. What's interesting to you about emails?"

"Emails are something I know how to do. I haven't ever sent a bulk email or whatever you call it. I've only ever sent emails from my personal account, but I know what they are. And I know how important they are. I didn't know much about creating webinars before we talked about them, so I had a lot more reservations. But now that we're back on familiar territory, I'm ready to dive right in."

"That's great to hear because emails are the lifeblood of any business," I said.

Emails fall into two categories:

1. Sequences, and
2. Regular newsletters

"You can leverage emails to build your list and therefore deliver 'warm' traffic to your site. The first step is to harness Michelle's enthusiasm about writing emails in the first place."

"Let's start with sequences. These are easier to write than you're thinking because you're going to write as if your reader didn't pay very close attention to your on-demand webinar."

"What do you mean by that?" Yosi asked. "Repeat ourselves?"

"That's exactly what I mean. Write one email for each step in your process or mistake, depending on the format your webinar took. This is where you'll be repeating yourself. That's good. People learn differently from text than they do from video, so even if it is *word for word* identical to what you discussed on video, having that content drip out over the next few days will help people feel connected to your topic and compelled to take the next step. Speaking of compelling people to take the next step, make sure you have a link to buy in every single email. 'Click here to join today' and link to your shopping cart. Spread out your links — sometimes put them near the beginning, sometimes at the end, sometimes as a PS — just make sure that every single email includes one call to action, and in this sequence, make sure that every email sends people to the same place."

"Hang on, that sounds like a lot of emails," Jackie said. "Let's say my offer has seven lessons. That's *eight emails*. That seems like spam!"

I nodded. "This hesitation comes up a lot and I want to address it in a bit, but remember: everyone on your list signed up on their own accord, which means they asked you to tell them more about how you can solve this problem for them. You're not going to send them one email a day for the rest of their lives. Once they're done in this sequence, they're done with daily emails from you. They get added to your regular newsletter."

## COMMIT TO WRITING AN EMAIL ONCE A WEEK TO YOUR LIST

Another place I see entrepreneurs hesitate is with sending weekly newsletters. And I completely understand because I get dozens of emails a day, and I'm not that important!

But I only get emails from people and businesses I want to hear from, and that's true for you too (hopefully).

So you're *not* bothering the people on your list. They *want* to hear from you.

There are a few different formats you can follow for your email newsletters, and the one you choose right now can be completely different from the one you eventually gravitate to. The simplest approach is one topic, one email, sent at the same time every week.

If there is just one piece of non-negotiable advice I can offer, it's to also make it regular. Email marketing is relatively simple: communicate regularly with your subscribers, let them see your humanity, and allow them a peek behind some not-quite-finished stuff. But if you're only talking to them once a month, you're no longer top of mind, and then you'll start equating sending emails with people unsubscribing from your emails, which is not the case when you send emails more frequently.

Of course, the converse is true as well: double check your email settings so that someone going through your sequences doesn't also get your newsletter because as much as I want you to connect with your audience, I do not want you to overwhelm them with your emails.

Finally, just remember that even if you make a mistake, I've made more than you. Just move on and don't allow a mistake or a mean-spirited reply derail you. You should not dread your email provider — it's there to connect you to the people who want to hear from you.

Not that we could forget, but we've been talking so long about the marketing engine and its fuel that you might have thought I'd forgotten all about content. Far from it, however — just saving the best for last. And since content is what Michelle, Yosi, and Jackie are all about, let's rejoin their conversation about content and the marketing engine.

# CREATING CONTENT
# (AND FIGURING OUT WHAT TO SAY)

"Creating content for your audience is so vital to getting people to come to your site that you might be surprised I waited until now to talk about it. But I've found that creative types struggle less with content once the delivery mechanism is in place. That said, just like everything else we've discussed, there's an easy way, and a hard way."

"Oh, I don't even want to hear about the hard way," Yosi said. "Can we talk about the easy way first?"

I smiled. "Yes, but with one important caveat: the easy way will feel hard at first."

Yosi groaned, so I gave her a reassuring smile.

"I want to ask a question. Which of you considers yourself a writer?" I asked.

They looked at each other. No one looked at me.

"Here's the thing I've discovered: I *do* consider myself a writer, but writing content is feeding a relentless beast with an unending hunger who will simply never get its fill. It used to be enough to simply churn out plenty of noise. Back in the bad old days, the site that wrote the most words, with the right combination of keywords, won the traffic awards. But there's a reason I call those the bad old days. To win the traffic awards, what everyone was doing was to fill the internet with garbage. As users and internet searchers, we don't want to have to sift through the garbage to get to the good stuff, but the other side of that coin is that in order to get the attention of search engines today, you have to write *substantial* posts. Your posts need to be long-form, the kind of content that takes hours upon hours to create. The average word count, according to those in the know, is 2000 words."

"Who can write that many words week after week?" Yosi asked, alarmed.

I nodded. "Even for people who identify as writers, that's *a lot* of words. And there's no guarantee that it'll work. But lucky for you, I've figured out an easier way."

"We are all ears," Jackie said.

"Great! Then let me tell you how to create talking head videos, where you speak for five to ten minutes on one of your topics."

"What? How on earth are videos the *easy* way?" Michelle asked, looking around the room as if to find a way to escape.

I smiled. "That's everyone's first reaction. But the truth is, people watch videos more than they read blog posts. And once you figure out how easy it is to create videos, you won't worry about creating content ever again. Because talking for five to seven minutes about a topic is so much easier than sitting down to write 2000 words about your topic. Let me take you through the process I use with my clients at my video content marketing agency."

They looked suspicious. Instead of charging forward, I paused a beat.

"Based on the looks on your faces, I think it might be helpful to voice your hesitations at the beginning so I can address them now. That way when I do go through my process you'll believe what I say. So let's hear them! I will stay silent while you list what's going through your minds right now, and I'll wait until you're done speaking before responding. You don't have to wait to be called on. Just go."

They did not disappoint. They responded, nearly speaking over each other, anxious to get their concerns out in the open.

"I don't have the right equipment!"

"I'm no good on camera!"

"I don't know what to say!"

"I can't hire a videographer!"

"What the heck should I do with my hands?"

"How do I edit?"

"Where do I put the videos?"

This went on for a few minutes, then they realized I was waiting for them to stop, and they settled down.

I stood up and picked up my fountain pen.

"I'm holding this object because it has magic powers," I started. They looked at me like I'd said that the Earth was flat.

"Are you just testing to see if we're still here if we're still paying attention?" Jackie asked with a smile.

I shook my head. "Not this time. Every time I record a video, I hold onto this pen. It helps me get my point across without me stammering. 3-year-olds have their stuffies, Linus had his blanket, I have my fountain pen. Your job is to find something like that, and you'll be fine."

"Rest assured that's not all I have to say about creating videos. We've been talking all weekend about building businesses based on the knowledge we already have. You're experts. Which means you can talk about your subject *all day long* if you were given the opportunity. Expert videos *allow* you to do that. Let me show you how we come up with topics for our client videos."

And then I handed out a piece of paper. Let me talk a little bit about what's on it because it's our guide to how we create video content with our clients. It has all the different prompts you'll ask yourself when you're getting started. Most of our clients already have a lot of content, so our research process is a little different with them, but the skeleton is still there if you understand the process I'm going to outline here.

The first section is devoted to answering questions.

- What questions do your customers ask?

- What questions do your prospects ask during sales conversations?

- And before you think this doesn't apply to you, what are the questions you WANT your customers to ask?

- What do you think your prospects should be asking during sales calls?

The next section is about competitors. We can learn a lot about what we should discuss in a video based on the things that our competition is doing. So, list a few examples of websites you think might be your competition.

The final section is about your lines in the sand. There are things you believe. They're the things that are your fundamental truths. They're the things that rile you up. Look to the thoughts you downloaded from your brain on day one for inspiration here. There's nothing more compelling than watching someone speak from their passions.

If you answer these questions fully you should easily have ten things in each section. And once you've answered these questions, you'll also start to feel your brain start running in the background. You'll find that topic ideas will come to you when you least expect them to. That's all it takes to create an outline of a *very robust* content marketing strategy.

Back to the discussion:

"When we work with clients, we pull out the list, and we ask which topic jumps out at them or where they'd like to start. They pick a topic and then we'll go over the main talking points. Then we ask them to select a call to action."

"This is a key point. Every video needs to send a viewer to a destination. What do you want people to do once they've finished watching? Where are you sending them? The calls to action are one of three things:

- Download a thing
- Book a call
- Buy a product

"Knowing before you hit the record button where you want to send your viewer is super helpful in informing *you* when to stop talking — when you've reached that point where it's natural to refer them to the action you want them to perform. And the only things you need to know before you record your video are; the topic or title, your main talking points, and your destination at the end."

"Let me be clear about what I'm asking for. Essentially all I'm after is you hitting the record button on your camera and talking into the camera explaining the topic. Imagine that you're having a conversation with someone — me, perhaps — and introduce the video as if someone *just* asked you the question you're going to spend the next five or six minutes explaining. Start with a story, lead to your points, don't talk too fast, and end with a compelling call to action."

Michelle scoffed. "Oh, that's all there is to it?"

I smiled. "It sounds like a lot," I said. "But you have a huge list of topics already, and after you record a few videos, you'll find that it's a much smoother process than trying to write that much down. Trust me."

"But there's so much more I think you need to know more than that," said Jackie. "I mean, there's quite a lot that goes into making a video besides what you're talking about. I know I can talk about plant-based eating till the cows come home. But that doesn't automatically translate into a usable video."

"So let's talk about that. Two things first: you hereby have my permission to trash your first two videos. And you do not need to aim for perfection here, so you do not have my permission to trash all of your videos. Now, are you ready to learn my process?"

Michelle looked a little less skeptical. "Sure," she said, and the others nodded.

"Great. This is all about tricking *ourselves* into creating a ton of content in a very condensed time period, and the first trick is to find someone to do this with you. Find a partner and do this together."

"What, you mean record our videos with the other people in this room?" Yosi asked. "I don't mean to be rude, but what if our topics don't have anything to do with each other?"

"That actually works to your advantage as you won't be worried about comparing your content to theirs. The point in working with someone else is to get them done. So here's how it'll work. Set a time to meet — and you can do this remotely — and take turns. Make sure you do the Mindstorming ahead of time and pick three or four topics that jump out at you. Then whoever goes first will start recording while their partner remains silent. You'll talk about your topic, you'll make eye contact with your friend who is muted, and you'll end with a call to action. When you are done, your friend does the same. Repeat this process until you run out of energy. And if you like how it goes, schedule another time to do this together in a month."

"You want us to coach each other?"

"Do we just record the call?"

"What about editing?"

I liked those questions. They were going to do it, they just needed to figure out the framework they needed to follow.

I smiled. "I'll send you home with the exact production checklist my team follows with every video we create, but let me review the points covered on it. You record your video locally on your own machine. Whatever comes built into the system you have will work just fine. Hit record when it's your turn to go and save it as high-quality as you can. Start with some light edits. It's worth it to learn how to do this because hiring professional video editors cost a lot more than you expect. The more videos you do, the less you'll have to edit because you won't lose your train of thought. But you will at first, so learning how to edit out your awkward bits is worth the investment of time and energy."

"Video editing sounds exhausting," Michelle said.

"It is and it isn't. It's worth learning, and there is a learning curve, but there's so much power in a well-edited video. You'll discover that technology today makes it easier than ever to edit a video. And once you've recorded a full video, all of a sudden you have a ton of content. The next step is to turn your spoken words into written ones, which you can then use as blog posts, emails for your newsletter, tweets, pithy messages on LinkedIn, and so on."

"And luckily for us, we live in the future where there are all kinds of apps that can help us with all of this."

"After you have the video and the blog post, it's time to repurpose. Add the captions back to the video file itself, then use your video editor to repurpose that video into the correct dimensions for your various social media platforms."

"You think we should add the captions to all our videos?" Yosi asked. I nodded. "The vast majority of people who watch videos on Facebook at least watch them on mute," I said. "So don't make people click a button. Just add the captions to all your videos."

"Hang on," Michelle said. "I'm not buying that statistic you just threw out there — what do you mean *most people* watch videos on mute?"

"It's true. According to a statistic from Buffer, more than 80% of videos on Facebook are watched without sound. And let's face it, there are many times where it makes sense to watch a video on mute: when you can't sleep but you're in a room with a sleeping person; when you've unplugged from your earphones for the day but you don't want to disturb anyone; or when you just don't want anyone around you to know that you're watching something with sound. When I told my dad this, he said that it might be true, but that someone like him always watches with sound, but with the captions on as well."

Yosi nodded, but Michelle and Jackie looked uneasy. "Adding captions is really easy," she told them. "Far easier than it sounds. I can show you in less than three minutes how I do it."

"Yosi's right," I said. "At first I thought it would be hard, but it's not."

"Really? Ok then — I trust the both of you if you say so," said Jackie.

"Here's where it gets fun," I told them. "You take that one video, where you talked for five to ten minutes, and you repurpose it so it goes *everywhere*. The greatest part about it is that it takes away any consideration of whether you need a different strategy for YouTube than LinkedIn. The process is straightforward. First, upload to YouTube. You want to have a presence on the things Google owns so you can get some search traffic. Next is the transcript. Embed the YouTube video into a blog post, turn the transcript into something people can read and search engines can index, then move on to social media."

There is one final point I'd like to make. Once you get your first few blog posts under your belt, you'll have a rhythm to put out and distribute as much content as necessary. You can schedule your social media posts to pull specific quotes from your blogs for six months after you hit publish. (There are too many different tools you can use to cover them all in the span of a short book, but in general, it's a good idea to outsource some of your promotion to robots so you have something posting on the major social networks at least once a day.) Then you can go about your life, document things on social media, and not have to think about promotion because you'll have it set up on a schedule.

By now I'm sure your head is spinning, but you're going to have to trust me when I say that everything I've described in fueling the marketing engine is significantly easier than it seems. It's all a matter of finding a process, figuring out what parts of it don't work for you, and making it your own. None of this is too technical to figure out — trust me because I did, and when I started I was even more of a novice than you are.

That's not to say that your feelings aren't real. Let's hear from the Mindshop participants on the things that concern them the most.

## HESITATIONS

I took a long look at all three women. They all looked pretty uncomfortable.

"Do you have any questions?" I asked.

Yosi was quiet and Jackie was fidgeting, so Michelle was the first to speak. "This seems like a lot of promotion. And — I don't want to speak for anyone else here — but I'm just not comfortable with this level of promoting myself."

Yosi and Jackie nodded in agreement.

"Oh," I said. "I understand. I'm sure it feels like a lot from where you're sitting. And what you're feeling is completely normal. There are mindset barriers that keep people from promoting their content, especially when that content is on a site with your name and your face. But these barriers will hold you back, so let's dive into them one by one."

"Let me walk you through what is very likely going to happen once you leave here. You're going to spend your days getting stuff done: getting your website right, creating your lead-generating opt-in, writing your emails, writing your sales pages, recording your videos, writing blog content, all of it. You'll get something ready to put out into the world, although you'll never feel like any part of it is 'done' necessarily, but what do you do once you feel ready? Or honestly, just before you feel ready? You promote it."

They continued to look uncomfortable. "Let me tell you a story about the olden times. The year was 2011. The internet was small. Heck, Twitter had only been around for three years. In those days, simply creating something as good as what you're about to create would have been enough. Search engines were hungry for excellent content. You could have published a few great pieces and then gotten media attention. Some people I know who started out in those days hit publish and got hundreds of thousands of page views immediately. Television stars were born."

"The bad news is those days are gone. The good news is that in the present, everyone has to promote their content. Since search engines don't play favorites, that levels the playing field, and now there's no such thing as 'pure' content. Everyone is promoting their content — you won't stick out like a sore thumb at all."

Michelle said, "How do I do it without feeling like one of those self-absorbed *selfie* people? Those headshots will be the first 'formal' pictures of me since my high school year-book photos. Now I'm supposed to just plaster them all over the internet?"

I nodded. "I get it. I remember having a conversation one November with a group of digital content creators. One said she would simply *not* want to send an email on Black Friday because she knew just how many emails she was going to receive and she didn't want to add to the noise. I called her out on that idea. Even though it's uncomfortable, you have to push through. Because your content is fantastic, everyone *needs* to see it. In fact, I'd like you to write that statement down, and look at it multiple times a day until you believe it."

The women were nodding but still had hesitant looks on their faces.

"Let me put it this way. The buyer's journey isn't about you. You're the creator. You have to create content that meets people where they are. And you have to promote it for where your audience is in terms of their readiness to talk to you. So send the Black Friday email. There's a reason other people are sending them, and the fact that your audience is getting a bunch of emails over Thanksgiving weekend should be a green light for you. People love deals and they're looking for yours."

"You're not clogging up the feeds of the people who need to hear from you. You're not spamming people. You didn't buy any email addresses. You earned those addresses by giving people what they wanted in exchange for their email addresses. If you believe that you will handle that responsibility with the gravity it deserves."

Now they were nodding. "I get what you're saying about responsibility," Jackie said. "Forgive me for saying so, but I'm still a little worried about the other side of the equation. I know I will give them good content. What worries me is that I'll get nothing back in return and get discouraged."

I looked up. "I hear you. But do your future self a favor and really embrace promotion. Your worries about it will fade once you get some engagement. People will find you, subscribe to your channels, and read your emails. Those are the people who want to see what you have to say. And if you post in places where your target audience hangs out, you're going to start seeing traction."

"Think of it like fishing. Your social media content is the bait on the hook, and the best bait in the world isn't going to get anyone to bite unless you fish where the fish are. And once you get some engagement, it's a strong dopamine hit. Because that first person — who isn't your mom or your sister — is going to help you push through the discomfort and give you the satisfaction you deserve. You're going to get people saying, 'thank you so much for this' or 'this is exactly what I needed to hear' and that will help you realize you're not simply spamming people."

"That helps," Yosi said. "But I'm having trouble with the idea that I'm some kind of expert."

I held my hand up to my mouth. "What?" I said, in mock disbelief. "You mean to tell me you've gotten all the way to day three without being able to confidently stand in your expertise?"

They laughed.

"I'm not making fun of you, Yosi. Imposter syndrome is a very real thing. And although there are ways to mitigate it, there's no way to 'get over' it, not in the long run. I think part of this comes from breaking through your comfort zone. You've committed to building on YourName.com, adding your headshots to the web, and you've downloaded a bunch of your ideas from your brain. So it might seem like what you're doing is bragging. Telling people you know all there is to know about everything. But that's not what people see when they come to your site."

I turned to her. "Let me ask you a question: do you know more about effective Instagram strategies than someone who's only logged in a few times?"

She nodded. "Yes, of course, I do."

"Great. Just keep that in mind. You are not telling people how to live their lives or what kind of mortgage to get. You are sharing your specific knowledge. You know a lot already and you're committed to keep learning. That means you'll always be ahead of your subscribers and always have something to share with them."

I turned to the group. "Everyone here has a deeper understanding of and connection to their topics than the people who need it. You're building your authority. More than that, you're demonstrating your authority through promotion that will let people know that you're more knowledgeable than the person in front of you at the coffee shop. You're creating content around and talking about a topic that you've been intimately familiar with for a long time now. You know more than a Muggle!"

I looked up. Their expressions were changing. I saw their hesitance melt, at least a little.

"This is another spot of hesitation that diminishes by the simple act of creating more content. When you start creating and distributing more content about your topic, in your voice, you are simply creating more authority for yourself — more proof that you can look to and say, yes, I *do* know more about that topic than I thought — and by extension, you're building more content for your audience. People will start coming to you and looking to you for advice and insight on your subject. And then, your credibility will increase in that space. All of a sudden, you'll become seen as an expert on your subject by the people who need to be convinced of your expertise."

Jackie was the one who responded this time. "Let me see if I understand what you just said: that in order to feel more like experts, we need to create content that proves, to us, that we are the experts you say we are?"

Michelle said, "That's what I understood. Because I don't feel like an expert at all. But if I had dozens of pieces of content, in my voice, talking about things I know, I'm pretty sure I would probably feel a bit different than I do two days after realizing that I actually know things."

"Exactly," I said. "The voice in your head is telling you that you have no right to call yourself an expert. But once you've written posts, recorded videos, answered questions, and had an archive you could point to, then you can tell that voice to pipe down. You can cite your sources. You'll be on pretty solid ground when you speak with that authority."

"Okay, that makes sense," Yosi chimed in. "Part of this feels like it'll always be a game to trick myself into pushing the walls of my comfort zone. But I'm not very outgoing, and I definitely do not want to be annoying."

"Actually, that's the next barrier I want to talk about," I said. "Not wanting to be annoying. That's a very noble aim. We've had decades of conditioning. Don't boast, don't be prideful, don't speak up, even the 'actions speak louder than words' adage is something that keeps people like us quiet. But staying quiet will keep you from getting in front of the clients you need to get in front of."

I had their attention now.

# ANNOYING THINGS
# ANNOYING PEOPLE DO AND SAY

"There's one thing I need to make clear," I said. "People who *are* annoying never worry about being annoying. So the simple fact that you don't want to be annoying means that you won't be. Saying you don't want to be annoying is the polite half of the sentence. The impolite part, the part we don't say out loud, and maybe we don't even say this part to ourselves, is that when we say we don't want to be annoying, we are picturing a real person we know who is annoying.

"Turn to a blank page in your notebook, and write, 'I don't want to be annoying like _____' at the top of the page. Write down the name of the person you have in mind when you think of someone annoying. What does that person do that annoys you? What do they say? How do they act? I'll give you just a few minutes to write down your thoughts."

They wrote for a bit. "You do not have to share names or details," I said, to bring them back into the room, "but look at your list of characteristics. What does an annoying person do? What does this specific person do that drives you crazy?"

"She talks about herself all the time," Michelle said.

"He just brags and brags and brags," Jackie said.

"They can't stop talking about themselves long enough to even ask me how I'm doing," Yosi said.

"I'll stop here because this is enough to get us started," I said. "Diving deeper into your frustrations won't be productive. But what is productive is simply knowing that if you follow the steps that we've been discussing you will not be annoying. You're not going to be bothering people. People will unsubscribe — that's an inevitability. But just because a friend who wasn't your target customer unsubscribed from your email list doesn't mean you were annoying. All it meant was that your message wasn't connecting with someone who wasn't in your target market anyway. Your target audience is waiting for you to produce more content. They want to learn from you. They want to laugh with you. They want to connect with you. They want to hit the like button to tell you to keep going."

"Most people in the world are content consumers. So if you can be a content producer, which you're committing to by building a business around your expertise, then quite literally no part of what you're doing is annoying. In fact, no part of the content distribution process is annoying. When you first start sharing your content in places where your audience hangs out, you're a fresh voice. An exciting point of view. A different take. That'll be where you start, and where you'll be for the first bit. But then, after you've been sharing for some time, your freshness wears off and gets replaced by something even better. You become the go-to voice. The expert. The authority. People come to you to see your content, and they stay to hear what you have to say. When something happens in your industry or the world at large, they're going to want your take."

I looked up. They looked interested instead of hesitant.

"Yosi, I'm going to put you on the spot. Can you tell me one of your favorite musicians?"

"Let's see, I'm all over the place with my musical love. But Lizzo is who I listen to when I need a boost of energy."

I turned to Michelle. "Who is one of your favorite contemporary writers?"

"I just finished a book by Zadie Smith," she replied.

"Let's say Lizzo drops a new record, or Zadie Smith publishes a new book," I said. "Would you want to know about it? And if you heard about it more than once, would you be annoyed or interested?"

"I get your point," Jackie said. "We'd be interested because we want to see and hear and read their content. The thing I'm having trouble with is thinking about becoming the kind of person who has people out there appreciating my content."

I stopped and looked at her. "That's the truest thing I've heard this weekend," I said. "That is a very brave and vulnerable thing to say. Thank you for that. And it's true that you're not Lizzo — who among us is? — but you will be seen as an expert by your target audience, and far sooner than you think. You'll get followers who will see you as the person they turn to for advice. The best part about this is that once you start doing it, you're going to find people out there who are going to be begging you for more. Pretty soon you'll stop worrying about what people will think about you if you start promoting your business because you'll be too busy sharing your expertise to recognize that you're promoting yourself by helping others."

"There's one last hesitation I want to address before we move on, and it's what I'm calling, for lack of a better phrase, not wanting to be THAT guy. We already wrote about the annoying person, but THAT guy is different. THAT guy is also quite annoying. He — not always he, but we'll use that pronoun — is always closing. Always asking for a sale too soon. Sees prospects as prey. THAT guy took all the lessons from what not to do as a salesperson and does them *all* the time. Can you picture THAT guy?"

"Ugh, yes!" Yosi said. "I do not want to be THAT guy. I want to be true to myself."

"So do I," Michelle said. "Same here," Jackie said.

I grinned. "Now I'm going to give you some different advice that's going to be the most uncomfortable advice you've gotten yet. Channel your inner THAT guy. The reason you hate THAT guy is because you're outside his target audience and you're seeing his stuff anyway. Aside from slightly off-targeting, THAT guy is pushing content into the right channels. THAT guy is testing channels. Testing different communities and groups to see where his target audience is and what kind of messaging connects with them. THAT guy is winning. And that's who I want you to channel. You can channel THAT guy while still being true to yourself."

"Your brand is how you portray yourself to the public, and it is not going to get diluted by creating and distributing your content. In fact, quite the opposite will occur. The more content you put out there, the better it will be. Channel the power of first draft publishing and put out content that you'll cringe at in a year."

"What are you waiting for? Once you channel your inner THAT guy and embrace the fact that you're creating things people are excited, anxious, over-the-moon thrilled to hear about the things you're putting out there, then it's simply a matter of executing the plan, and letting automation tools help you."

# CONCLUSION

I looked at the clock. It was nearing the end of the day.

"We covered *a lot* this weekend," I told them. "We downloaded ideas out of our brains. We talked about different ways to look at income and revenue, and we started building the framework of the marketing engine you'll build. That's a lot of ground, and once you leave here your head just might be spinning."

Jackie laughed. "I don't have to wait to leave for my head to spin!"

Michelle chuckled. "Me neither!"

Yosi gestured to the pile of papers she'd amassed over the past few days. "I don't know what you're all talking about," she said, grinning. "All this seems 'fine'!"

I smiled at them all.

"Here's the thing: we've created a whole new way to think. Once you get home, it's normal to feel a little 'hungover' from all the information you've drunk in. But what I want you to remember is that these past few days were not a dream. What we learned and what you started to build is real. It's there ready for you to execute. But you have to take the next step. I've seen people go through these weekends and mentally leave what they learned here. They fly home, then pack all the work they got through into a notebook or a binder or a place on their hard drive that never gets touched again. Then, one day, a few months down the road, they'll stumble upon it, maybe when they're decluttering or they need their suitcase for something else. They'll sit down with the material and realize just how much they had and wonder where their momentum went."

I looked searchingly at each of them.

"I don't want that for you. What you have now is a seedling. With the right kind of care, that seedling will grow into something beautiful. But if you abandon your ideas and don't nurture them, what will happen is as predictable as what happens to a neglected seedling — it'll wither. Your ideas can't live without your care. So before we go, I want to give you some tools that you can refer back to once you're back home with other competing priorities. Ready?"

They nodded. "Let's say, right now, what each of you will focus on after you get home. It's not a contract, per se, as much as it is committing to the pursuit of one idea. Yosi, do you want to start?"

She nodded. "I'm going to put together a coaching program that will help people learn how to tell compelling stories through Instagram. Videos and stills." She turned to Jackie.

"I'm excited to build my coaching program too! I'm going to help the veggie-curious add more plants to their lives in a one-on-one setting," Jackie said.

Michelle was quiet. "Where do you think you'll start, Michelle?" I asked.

"I'm not sure," she replied. "I think maybe I'll put together a workshop on the clean-enough house concept. But don't hold me to it."

You're likely at the same starting point as Jackie, Michele, and Yosi as well.

The first thing I want to caution you about is **analysis paralysis**. If you've been diligently doing the Mindstorms like the group, then you likely have a pile of papers as tall as the one Yosi has. On every one of those sheets of paper, there is at least one task you need to perform once you get home. Taken as a whole, it's overwhelming. What are you to do?

My advice is simple: don't take them as a whole. Commit to doing one thing per day. Don't commit to ten because it'll be too easy to give up. As someone's great-great-grandfather used to say, the way to eat an elephant is one bite at a time.

I have mentioned **imposter syndrome** before as it often crops up even when you're doing the initial Mindstorms, but undoubtedly once you step away from this work for enough time, you'll start to forget about your brilliance. You'll read about something someone else is doing and you'll want to chase that instead of the ideas you downloaded from your brain. Worse yet, you'll start to think everyone else is brilliant and you're not. The devil on your shoulder is sitting there, telling you that you don't have what it takes. That you can't do this. That you were under a spell thinking you could while completing the Mindshop, but that in the cold light of day, your ideas are trash.

I want to say two things about this. The first is to talk back to the devil on your shoulder. Your ideas are not trash: in fact, your ideas are going to make the world a better place. But they can't make a difference if they only exist in your head. This is again not motivational poster talk: your ideas will undoubtedly help those they are meant to serve. The challenge is developing them into an economically viable idea that can be successfully marketed. But never doubt for a second the worth of your ideas. That's not up for debate.

The second point I want to make is this: we all have friends. Some are business friends and others are just personal friends. If you really want to carry through on these ideas, make yourself accountable. Tell your friends what you are up to and specifically ask them to (gently) badger you about your progress. There's not a workout plan in the world that's not more successful without some sort of accountability: the same is true of making sure work plans turn out.

If you're not paralyzed by thoughts of being an imposter, then the thing you have to fear next is the **slow death** of your ideas from lack of momentum. If you're anything like me, you'll start to lose steam on some of your ideas. But in truth, chances are, that if you doubled down instead of giving up, you'd see the needle move. That's why the quarterly experiments are so important — you get to see fairly quickly whether an idea has traction. You set your metrics, decide where to focus your attention, and see if you can get traction.

This is a good idea for a second reason as well. It ensures that you're devoting your time to ideas that are going to work. This way you're not just chasing something that seems like a good idea but turns out to simply be a distraction. For me, it's a way to acknowledge my squirrel-like attention span instead of trying to stifle my natural tendencies. Remember, they call it shiny object syndrome for a reason: we chase things that gleam in the distance because what's in front of us looks dull and gray and ... a lot like work. This way I get the best of both worlds: I make my quarterly goal clear, test one idea on one market, and in a reasonable amount of time I can see what has potential and what was just a distraction.

And here was my final piece of advice to the three women at the Mindshop.

"This is going to sound completely ridiculous," I said, sheepishly. "But it's helpful to think of yourself as the hero of your own epic story.

"Here's the thing about epics. They are made up of shorter, individual episodes, but those episodes are part of a long quest. There's nothing contradictory in saying, 'chart your course, stay the path, make it matter,' and tell you to do it one quarter at a time."

"Nor do I want you to think I'm talking out of both sides of my mouth when I say zoom out and take the long view. Think about yourself in ten years. One of the ways I do this is by doing a bit of disassociation. I have three Kathleens: past-Kathleen, who did some things right but a lot of things wrong, today Kathleen, who I simply refer to as myself, and future-Kathleen, who is the person I'm trying to do nice things for."

"Here's how this works for me in action: When I come home from vacation to a clean house with a made bed, I thank past-Kathleen for the work she did to make coming home wholly positive. When I go to yoga, drink enough water, and put on sunscreen, I tell myself that future-Kathleen will thank me one day."

"Taking the long view changes *everything*: the way I approach business, sure, but also the way I approach things like fitness. I no longer kill myself in the gym or allow myself to get dragged to circuit training because the answer to 'Will

I be doing this to my body in ten years?' is almost invariably no. It helps with shiny objects, which is one of the most damaging parts of running your own show. You'll see an example about how someone did something completely unrelated to the thing you want to build, and for a moment you'll visualize yourself over there. But ask yourself: do I want this to be where my life goes in ten years? And let the answer guide your next move."

"That was my last piece of business advice, but I do want to end with a piece of personal advice. When you're building your body of work based on your own expertise and knowledge, the easiest thing in the world to do is overwork yourself to the point of sickness. My husband likes to joke that I'm addicted to 'workahol', and I'm guessing you all are too, or you wouldn't be at a retreat like this."

"That said, here are my tricks for staying healthy. One: exercise at a set time every day, and put it on your calendar. Build your entire schedule around it, because if you don't, you'll talk yourself into doing anything other than exercise. This is the one thing that has led me to commit to a daily yoga practice. Another thing about staying healthy that is harder is to rest. Understand that resting is essential to creative work. It's not a reward you get at the end of the day if you've done all the right things. It's the opposite side of the work coin. Add rest to your days as well. Keep the long game in mind. Make the best decision for you in ten years, not you at the moment."

Arguably the most important thing about being you is that you have a choice. You have a choice when you put down this book. You can decide to leave behind the work that you did to get to this point or leave it locked in memory, trapped in amber. Or you can decide to start.

The methods and techniques I've gone over in this book have worked for hundreds of other people just like you. They turned their thoughts and ideas into viable businesses. With this program as a blueprint, there's nothing standing in your way except fear.

Thank you for taking the time to read my book. I wish you all the best with your ideas. I know I'll be hearing about them soon.

# ACKNOWLEDGEMENTS

Thank you to: my husband, Brent, my first reader, first everything. My business partner, Emma Bates, who believed in this project before I did. My incomparable editor, D. Olson Pook, who told me that the pile of words I'd written were in fact a book, and who took care to re-organize everything to prove to me that this was so. My friend and mastermind partner, Erin Donley, who gave the kind of feedback only someone who ghostwrites three books a year could give. My friend Anne Keery, who made me a chart and told me to write and write and write. Terri Trespicio, for holding a writing retreat and assuring me that I had a book in me, and for holding session after session of Gateless writing salons that helped me complete it. Everyone in those salons who encouraged me and promised to buy a copy. My sister, Caitlin Bird, who lifted me up in ways she'll never even know, on the days I needed it most. My dad, Mike O'Malley, who has always been an extraordinary proofreader, and made the book better with each suggestion. The Thought Leaders in Australia who suggested that everyone has ten books in them. My best friend, Ashley Graves, who gave encouragement and believed that this book could become a reality. All my clients, past, present and future. Finally, my daughters, Clara and Parker, who are the reason I do any of this in the first place.

# RESOURCES

INTRODUCTION:

Download the workbook at MINDSTORMSbook.com

PART 2:

Pomodoro Timer: https://pomofocus.io/

PART 3:

It can be difficult to think about giving a talk, so start here for some of my favorites:

Stop searching for your passion | Terri Trespicio | TEDxKC

The skill of self-confidence | Dr. Ivan Joseph | TEDxRyersonU

How to Have a Good Conversation | Celeste Headlee | TEDxCreativeCoast

PART 4:

We go into a lot more depth about the layout and writing of sales pages in our Copy Blocks course. Learn more about that here: doingmarketingdifferently.com/copy-blocks/

PART 5:

We go into a lot more depth about the format for a webinar in our Webinar Blocks course. Learn more about that here: https://doingmarketingdifferently.com/webinar-blocks

Access the **Remote Video Checklist** here: amplifiednow.com/checklist

Beautiful.ai for webinar slide decks

Made in the USA
Middletown, DE
09 October 2021

49962698R00130